Praise for the *Small Business Survival Book*

"... SCORE's goal is to help as many businesses as possible grow and succeed . . . this book is a great resource guide for all small businesses and startup's alike . . ."

—Ken Yancey, CEO, SCORE Association

"The *Small Business Survival Book* is the ultimate guide for entre-preneurs who are serious about success."

—Karen Kerrigan,
President and CEO,
Small Business & Entrepreneurship Council
Founder, Women Entrepreneurs Inc. (WE Inc.)

Small Business Survival Book

12 Surefire Ways for Your Business to Survive and Thrive

Barbara Weltman
and
Jerry Silberman

WILEY

John Wiley & Sons, Inc.

Published by John Wiley & Sons, Inc., Hoboken, New Jersey.
Published simultaneously in Canada.

For general information on our other products and services or for technical support, please contact our Customer Care Department within the United States at (800) 762-2974, outside the United States at (317) 572-3993 or fax (317) 572-4002.

Designations used by companies to distinguish their products are often claimed by trademarks. In all instances where the author or publisher is aware of a claim, the product names appear in Initial Capital letters. Readers, however, should contact the appropriate companies for more complete information regarding trademarks and registration.

Wiley also publishes its books in a variety of electronic formats. Some content that appears in print may not be available in electronic books. For more information about Wiley products, visit our web site at www.wiley.com.

Library of Congress Cataloging-in-Publication Data:

Weltman, Barbara, 1950-
    Small business survival book : 12 surefire ways for your business to
survive and thrive / Barbara Weltman and Jerry Silberman.
        p. cm.
    Includes index.
    ISBN-13: 978-0-471-75368-1 (pbk.)
    ISBN-10: 0-471-75368-8 (pbk.)
    1. Small business—United States—Management.   2. New business
enterprises—United States—Management.   3. Success in business—United
States.   I. Silberman, Jerry, 1961-   II. Title.
    HD62.7.W46   2006
    658.02'2—dc22

                                                                2005029365

Printed in the United States of America.

10 9 8 7 6 5 4 3 2 1

CONTENTS

INTRODUCTION

Americans have the entrepreneurial spirit and it is contagious. A March 2005 Gallup poll showed that 57 percent of citizens would prefer to start their own businesses, and, in fact, each year more than half a million new businesses open their doors. These owners start out as optimists, betting some or all of their financial resources and committing many hours of their time to their fledgling companies with the belief that they will succeed. Today, there are an estimated 45 million small businesses and self-employed individuals nationwide.

Unfortunately, despite the highest hopes and the best of intentions, almost as many businesses fold each year as those that start up. Poor sales, natural disasters, and mounting debt are some of the key reasons why nearly 50,000 firms go out of business each month and why 18,000 each month go bankrupt.

So what makes some companies succeed while others fail? It's a given that things will happen: Your key salesperson goes to your competitor; your bank changes its lending policies, leaving you out in the cold; or a flood damages your inventory. It's *how* you deal with these and other events that makes the difference between staying afloat and going under.

You need a lot of different things to make your business work. First and foremost, you need the right attitude to run your business effectively. As a business owner, you're forced to wear many different hats. Not only do you have to handle the core of your business—consulting, medicine, construction, retailing, or whatever type of business you're in—you also have to oversee the company's finances, personnel, marketing, purchasing, and many other tasks. In effect, you must learn how to wear all your different hats well.

Depending on your type of business, you need an internal workforce that can meet the demands of your business. A small business is very demanding of its employees because each person is critical to the operation, and you have to select people who can thrive in this type of environment.

Regardless of whether you work alone or have a staff, you need to assemble of team of experts to help you each step of the way—from start-up through expansion, through hard times and crises. No matter how much you think you know, you should at least recognize that you can't know it all and will turn to an outside professional, such as an attorney, accountant, banker, insurance agent, or other expert, for help.

You need to make plans for all contingencies and remain nimble so you can react to changing events. From safeguarding your company's secrets to insuring against theft and other losses, you must treat your business as a precious gem to be carefully and diligently protected. And should disaster strike, you want to be able to react appropriately and save the day.

You need to operate your business in such a way as to stay on top of obligations and critical information so you don't fall behind and find yourself in trouble. You can't let collection of your accounts receivable slide or fail to file tax returns when due. Much of this work is *not* intuitive, none of it is easy, and all of it is mandatory for a successful business.

Owning a business can be a fulfilling and financially rewarding career, but you need the tools to navigate life's uncertainties and problems. That's what this book is for—to guide you at any stage of your business through the rocks and shoals that you are bound to be in danger of washing up against. You'll learn how to be prepared for the worst and what to do if, in fact, you're faced with overwhelming problems.

Part One addresses the human side of business. This part is all about you and the people you work with. You can have the greatest product or service to offer the public, but if you don't surround yourself with equally great people—staff, contractors, advisers—your business probably won't last long.

Part Two explains the financial side of business. One of the key reasons why businesses fail is falling short of cash needed to pay monthly bills, so you must learn to monitor your cash flow. This may entail upgrading your collection activities so you extend credit wisely and get paid for what you do, or restructuring your debt to ease off your cash flow demands. Of course, you want to grow your business, which will bring in more cash, and this can be done effectively only if you plan your marketing strategies.

Part Three explores the unexpected side of business. You can bet the ranch on the fact that something unexpected always happens. But you can arm yourself against these eventualities with various legal and insurance protections. You can map out plans to follow in case of catastrophe.

Throughout the book you'll see how real small-business owners have faced problems, and you'll learn about the solutions that worked for them—and can work for you. You'll find resources to help you in every stage of your business. Many of the resources are online (be aware that web sites can change).

PART ONE

THE HUMAN SIDE OF BUSINESS

Adjust Your Attitude

Success or failure in business is caused more by mental attitude than by mental capacities.

—Sir Walter Raleigh

Most small-business owners were once employees of another company. That's how they learned their trade. That's how they decided to go it alone and become independent, working for themselves rather than for someone else. So why do so many small businesses fail to make it, with nearly half of them out of business within two years of opening their doors?

It's easy to make excuses, blaming the economy, the fact that a large chain store with which you compete has located in your area, that storms hampered your sales, or that you didn't get the breaks you expected. But excuses don't cut it. While a bad economy may push some businesses under, an equal if not greater number of small businesses make it nonetheless. Tangible events don't tell the whole picture.

The problem for many small-business owners is that in their heads they do not really make the transition from being an architect or a chef to owner of an architectural firm or a restaurant. They never grasp the distinction between being a great worker and a savvy business owner. They never go from being a worker to an owner.

According to Michael Gerber, author of The E-Myth, hopeful entrepreneurs start out with great zeal but little real focus on what it takes to be a successful business owner. To paraphrase him, gripped by the entrepreneurial desire, talented workers make the fatal assumption that by understanding the technical work of a business they understand the business that does that technical work. Wrong!

In this chapter you will see how false assumptions, unrealistic expectations, and Pollyanna attitudes can lead to disaster. You need more than a positive attitude to make your business work. You need the right attitude. This chapter explains how you can develop the right thinking and puts forth the actions to take to support that thinking in order to transform yourself into a capable business owner.

Develop Your Mind-Set

If you want to make it in your own business, you need to develop the right mind-set. Pretend your mind is like an Etch A Sketch that you can turn upside down to make it go blank. Erase your assumptions about what it takes to succeed in business. You don't need to be the smartest person in the world. You don't need to come from a family with connections. You don't need a Rockefeller's bankroll behind you. What you do need first and foremost is the right mind-set.

Now, with your mind a clean slate, start to build step-by-step (with our help) the right attitude for your business to succeed. Don't expect that a single reading of the following pages will magically transform you into the entrepreneur you hope to become. We can give you the information. But you have to live it to make it so.

Shoulder Responsibilities

One aspect of creating the right attitude is recognizing the broad range of responsibilities you must take on when you own a business. Instead of wearing one hat—say the hard hat of a construction worker—you must wear multiple hats at the same time when you become a home remodeling contractor. As a small-business owner, you are responsible for *every* aspect of the business for which a large company maintains separate departments. These include such activities as:

- Collections—staying on top of unpaid accounts receivable.

- Competitive intelligence—monitoring what your competitors are doing.

- Customer service—dealing with postpurchase issues and making the customer's experience with your company pleasurable in order to avoid problems and to generate repeat business as well as referrals.

- Finance—keeping track of the income and expenses of your business and paying taxes.

- Human resources (HR)—hiring, training, managing, and, when necessary, firing your staff.

- Information technology (IT)—keeping technology humming, including web site management, and avoiding IT problems such as online theft.

- Legal—complying with local, state, and federal government regulations to operate within the law.

- Marketing—gaining recognition and credibility in potential markets, advertising, public relations, strategic alliances, and joint ventures.

- Purchasing—buying the things you need at the right price to run your business, including inventory, supplies, and services.

- Sales—pitching your products or services to potential buyers.

- Strategic planning—setting sights on future projects and activities, including research and development for certain types of businesses, as well as disaster recovery planning for unfortunate events.

Are you prepared to wear all of these department head hats? Even if you have co-owners and capable employees, don't forget where the buck stops—it stops with you. Are you good at any of these separate activities, such as handling money or personnel? Are you a good salesperson? A smart buyer? A creative strategic planner? You don't necessarily have to excel at all of these jobs (though it wouldn't hurt), but you can't ignore any of them.

Take Things Seriously

One luncheonette owner in the New York City suburbs stocks penny (now nickel and quarter) candy in bins to entice neighborhood children to patronize her establishment. Moneywise, the candy adds little to her revenue, and children are not her prime patrons so their business isn't key to her company's success. Still, she spends many precious hours each week stocking her bins and reordering candies, an activity that she views as a hobby. The time and effort devoted to this nonproductive hobby could be better spent on promoting her profit center—the sandwiches.

This small-business owner is not alone in misdirecting her limited resources into fun, but not wise, business activities. The lesson here is again the mind-set. You can certainly have a hobby on the side, but running a business is a serious, profit-driven endeavor. You can't afford to be a dilettante when it comes to running a business. You need a professional attitude.

Focus

Your store hours may be 9 to 5. Your doors may be closed on Sundays or Mondays. But your mind can never be out to lunch. You have to be able to juggle the other demands that you may face—caring for children, training for the marathon, or participating in civic activities. The term *multitasking* doesn't begin to describe the job of being a small-business owner. Your business and personal lives often melt together, but you can't lose sight of your role in the business if you want this aspect of your life to succeed.

When you are at business, you must concentrate on the business challenges at hand. It's easy to become distracted with other aspects of your life, especially when family illness or other personal crises arise. But concentration on business matters is essential. When you face a major crisis—your computers are down or the delivery you needed today did not show up—it can become easy to concentrate fully on handling the immediate problem. But you need this same attention to business when things are humming, so that future crises can be averted.

Banish Negativity

The power of positive thinking is no myth. You need a positive view of things in order to make your business work. You're bound to hear naysayers' reasons why you won't succeed. After all, what makes you think you can make it when so many other businesses do not? Think about that restaurant location around the corner that seems to have a different owner every time you look. The naysayer will tell you that your restaurant will undoubtedly suffer a similar fate. Don't be dissuaded by this possibility alone.

You must tell yourself why you can make your business work, keeping your focus positive. To paraphrase Abraham Lincoln, most people are as successful as they make their minds up to be.

Here are some great ways to stay positive:

- *Visualize success.* In the words of scholar, pastor, and teacher William Arthur Ward (1921–1997), "If you can imagine it, you can achieve it; if you can dream it, you can become it." Simply put, if you *think* your business can succeed, then it can.

- *Stay away from negative people.* Negativity is contagious. Like a yawn that you see, hearing negative statements can make you and your employees also think negatively. Surround yourself instead with positive thinkers.

- *Stay flexible and adapt.* Things happen over which you have no control. Accept the fact that your key supplier may go out of business, your most valued employee will someday quit, a snowstorm will prevent a delivery, and so on. You can always find another supplier or another employee. You can make a delivery at another time. It's a given that despite your best efforts, you'll lose customers. It's a possibility that you can be robbed or fire can damage your location. The point is to remain nimble and make the best of unanticipated situations that are sure to arise.

- *Put the past behind you.* Negativity can grow if you let yesterday's mistakes fester. You don't want to ignore problems you've made, but you can't let them drive you toward the negative side of the street. Flip any mistake you've made into a positive thought that that's just one less mistake to make in the future. Learn from your mistakes and, most importantly, never make the same mistake twice. Self-help and salesmanship pioneer Dale Carnegie said, "When fate hands you a lemon, make lemonade."

- *Recognize small accomplishments.* Reinforce your positive attitude by recognizing each day how you've moved ahead. Pat yourself on the back for all the cold calls you've made or the one tough sale you've closed.

- *Be brave.* Being a business owner means you're a risk taker. You well understand that the decisions you make may not always produce the results you want. The new item you added to your product line that you had high hopes for may sit on your shelves. The person you hired to be your company rep may not work out. You cannot let setbacks and failures thwart your future risk taking. Your attitude must continue to include risk taking, so you must continue to be brave.

Fix Your Goals

Thinking isn't doing. And, for many people, it may not be possible to simply put yourself into a business owner frame of mind because we tell you to. But your behavior can help to alter this. If you *act* in a businesslike way, you start to *think* like a business owner. Transform your business mind-set into actions. The best way to do this is to fix goals for yourself.

You want to succeed, of course. Everyone who goes into business wants to succeed. But this desire is not a goal. This is just a desire. Don't confuse desire or motive with a goal. Take the following test to see if you know the difference between a desire and a goal. Here's a list of seven wants. Which ones can you identify as goals?

1. Being your own boss.

2. Setting your own hours.

3. Protecting your income from corporate downsizing.

4. Gaining prestige in your community.

5. Creating a business for your children to inherit.

6. Selling $50,000 in product in the first year.

7. Collecting fees for professional services of $100,000 by the second year.

If you chose any of the first five answers, you picked a desire rather than a goal. These are your hopes and dreams that can result if you can stay in business. In effect, they are the by-products of achieving your goals. Only answers 6 and 7 are goals. A goal, then, is a concrete objective. It is something that can be quantified and measured.

Why are goals important? Great achievers in all disciplines know the value of setting goals. Just ask a world-class runner who tries to beat his last best time by a few seconds how important a goal can be.

Setting Your Goals

Where is your business today? Where do you see it in six months? One year? Three years? Write down your goals for these time periods. Goals can include sales revenues, the number of new customers, the number of new locations, and any other objective that you can put a number on so you can measure it.

Goals should be realistic. Who doesn't want sales of $1 million or $10 million? And it's a good idea to aim high and fall short rather than to aim low and miss the opportunity to do more. But your goals should be in line with reasonable expectations. Work backwards. If you are a consultant and want to increase your revenue for the coming year from $75,000 to $150,000 (a goal that may or may not be reasonable), how many hours of work does this require? How much would you have to charge for your work to attain your goal? Working backwards can give you a better idea of your goal's feasibility. Maybe you realize you can't double your rates to reach your goal. But you may be able to raise them a little—and adjust your goal accordingly.

If your goal seems too lofty, it may be possible to break it down into manageable pieces. For example, instead of trying to increase sales by $10,000 per month, set a goal of increasing your daily sales by $500 (assuming there are 20 working days in the month). This more modest goal may be easier to attain on a day-to-day basis than aiming for the total $10,000 increase in one shot.

Commit Your Goals to Writing

Statistics demonstrate that writing down goals gives you an 80 percent edge on achieving them over those who do not put their goals in writing. Goals are really just the tip of the iceberg you can see; your business plan, which includes your goals, is the entire floe.

What does a business plan have to do with your attitude? Having a business plan can help to shape your attitude. It shows you are serious about being in business. You've taken the time to think through all aspects of your business and committed them to writing.

There are several other reasons why it's important to have a business plan. If you want commercial financing, you need to show a prospective lender your plan. You can't get a loan in most situations without it.

It can also be helpful for certain tax matters. Having a business plan is one of the key things that the Internal Revenue Service (IRS) uses to distinguish a business from a hobby activity. A business can deduct *all* of its expenses (with certain limits) while a hobby activity cannot deduct expenses in excess of income.

Writing a Business Plan

You don't have to be an Ernest Hemingway to write a business plan. You don't have to be a great typist or a computer genius. All you need is a good understanding of what a business plan is all about and the will to follow through.

Essentially a business plan is a description of your company today and where you expect it to be at a fixed point in the future (say three years). The owner of a start-up greeting card company in the Midwest was able to create a sufficient business plan in just two typed pages for a bank to give her a loan. The plan should include an explanation of each of the following points:

- A summary description of your business—its name and address, products or services, and your objectives for the future. This section is sometimes called an executive summary (even though no executives are mentioned in it).

- What your business does—its activities for producing revenue.

- The type of business organization—a limited liability company, an S corporation, and so on.

- Who owns the business—who you are, your background, and what you do for the company.

- Who runs the business—you and your team.

- The market you're in and the competition you face.

- What you need in order to operate—your office, store, factory, equipment, and the like.

- How much you make today (typically stated in terms of revenue based on sales) and what you expect to earn in three years, five years, and so on.

Money, of course, is a key element to your plan. If you're just starting out and haven't opened your doors, your plan should include a projection of start-up costs. Start-up costs include the price of everything you need to open your doors, from rent and equipment to inventory and insurance. Most importantly, the projection should include what you'll need to live on while your business gets going—something that could take months or even a year or two. If you're already in business, obviously you can skip start-up costs and focus on current needs.

If you're not a numbers person, you probably want to work with your accountant to prepare the financial parts of the plan. Doing this will help you assess whether the things you are doing now are really working for you. For example, you may be losing money on some products while making money on others. Putting the numbers together can give you a better idea of where you stand and help you develop a game plan for the future.

If you're preparing the business plan for your own use as a road map for future business growth, you can be as abbreviated as you want so long as you include all the information to gain a full picture of your company. The point is to get your mind into a business framework. But if you will be showing the business plan to outsiders (e.g., for financing), then you need to include a great deal of financial information and supporting documents.

For example, you need balance sheets and cash flow statements as well as copies of tax returns, leases, contracts, and the like.

There are many ways to get your business plan completed. You can employ a professional whose job is to draft business plans. For example, MasterPlanz (www.masterplanz.com) is a company of professional business plan writers; it charges from about $1,200 for a business looking for Small Business Administration (SBA) financing to $15,000 for a business looking for venture capital.

However, if you want to do it yourself, there are a number of resources you can use for a writing business plan. In addition to many books on the subject, there are also several online sites that can help.

RESOURCES

- Bplans.com from Palo Alto Software (www.bplans.com). View sample business plans that you can adapt to your business. Purchase software to develop and customize your own business plan. Cost: Business Plan Pro Standard is $99.95; Premier edition is $199.

- Business Resource Software (BRS) (www.brs-inc.com and click on "Business Plan"). There are three business-plan versions, with cost ranging from $49.95 to $219.95; the version to use depends on the purpose of your plan (e.g., commercial financing).

- Small Business Administration (www.sba.gov/starting _business and click on "Starting Your Business"). The SBA has an outline you can use to create your own business plan. It is divided into four sections: description of the business, marketing, finances, and management. You can follow the outline step-by-step to include all the necessary elements of a business plan. There are also sample plans for your review.

How do you know if your plan is on target and you've done a good job? You can have your plan reviewed free of charge by SCORE, Counselors to America's Small Business (www.score.org). This is a volunteer organization under the auspices of the Small Business Administration. Call your local chapter to schedule an appointment.

Create a Mission Statement

A business plan is like your sky map to help you navigate the heavens. But a mission statement is your guiding star. You need to be able to define for yourself and for the marketplace why your business exists, the things you value, and what you hope to accomplish. You know your mission statement is working if the public gets it and can understand your business.

If you can encapsulate these ideas in a sentence or two or be able to state your purpose in 30 seconds, you've got your mission statement. It can be a slogan running just one sentence, as do some from some well-known companies you probably recognize:

- Federal Express (FedEx): "We will produce outstanding financial returns by providing totally reliable, competitively superior, global, air-ground transportation of high-priority goods and documents that require rapid, time-certain delivery."

- Mary Kay Cosmetics: "To give unlimited opportunity to women."

- 3M: "To solve unsolved problems innovatively."

- Walt Disney Company: "To make people happy." (*Note:* There is a movement spearheaded by Roy Disney, the founder's nephew, to create a new mission statement.)

- Wal-Mart: "To give ordinary people the chance to buy the same things as rich people."

Most mission statements, however, are two, three, or four sentences long and include moral and ethical considerations, target markets, the products or services provided, and expectations of growth.

- IBM: "Our goal is simply stated. We want to be the best service organization in the world."

- McDonald's: "McDonald's vision is to be the world's best quick service restaurant experience. Being the best means providing outstanding quality, service, cleanliness, and value, so that we make every customer in every restaurant smile."

- Westin Hotels and Resorts: "In order to realize our Vision, our Mission must be to exceed the expectations of our customers, whom we define as guests, partners, and fellow employees. (mission) We will accomplish this by committing our shared values and by achieving the highest levels of customer satisfaction, with extraordinary emphasis on the creation of value. (strategy) In this way we will ensure that our profit, quality, and growth goals are met."

Writing Your Mission Statement

Usually a mission statement is extracted from the executive summary of your business plan. However, you can write your own statement independent of your business plan. In writing your mission statement, keep these points in mind:

- Describe who you are (what your company does) and why you exist.

- State your values and/or beliefs.

- Include your vision for the future. Steer clear of lauding your current accomplishments (e.g., providing great quality or service). You can reach for the stars. For example, in 1950, Boeing's mission statement was to "Become the dominant player in commercial aircraft and bring the world into the jet age"—a mission that seemed very ambitious at the time.

- Believe in what you write.

There are also online tools you can use to help create your own mission statement.

RESOURCES

- Bplans.com from Palo Alto Software (see earlier box) lets you view sample mission statements for free.

- Drucker Foundation's Leader to Leader Institute (from famed management expert Peter Drucker, www.pfdf.org and enter "Mission Statement" in the search box) has a 10-step article to help you develop your own mission statement.

- MissionExpert (www.missionexpert.com) sells software that guides you through a structured process to create and implement a mission statement. Cost: $24.95.

- Workplace Toolbox (www.workplacetoolbox.com) can write your statement for you. Cost: $389 for membership that includes other business services.

Remember that your mission statement isn't static. You can and should rewrite it as times change, you achieve initial objectives, or the company moves in a new direction. For example, Ford Motor Company's initial mission statement in the early 1900s was "Ford will democratize the automobile"; today it is "To become the world's leading consumer company for automotive products and services." Microsoft's initial mission statement was "To empower people through great software—any time, any place, and on any device"; today it is "We work to help people and businesses throughout the world realize their full potential." Review your statement annually to make sure it complies with what your company is still all about, and update it when you have achieved your company's initial mission or have simply changed direction.

Review Progress Regularly

Don't find yourself on the road to hell with all your good intentions. Make sure you translate your intentions into actions that will head you in the *right* direction. Just because you set goals doesn't mean you can sit back and do nothing further. You probably know a neighbor who started to finish his basement . . . years ago. He had a goal (a finished basement) and was a great starter. Unfortunately, he wasn't a finisher.

The actions discussed in this chapter are not a one-time affair. You should continually monitor your attitude. As things arise to cause setbacks, you can easily lose sight of staying positive and remaining focused.

Your goals should also be readjusted on a regular basis. It's common to fix new sales goals every quarter, for example. But your overall goals, besides sales, may benefit from a regular review as well. Compare your goals with your achievements at least once a year.

Keep Your Sense of Humor

Even though business is a serious matter, don't take yourself *too* seriously. Keep things light and you'll enjoy yourself more. You're bound to face disasters, but if you can laugh a little, things won't seem so bad.

You don't have to be Jay Leno, Chris Rock, or Ellen DeGeneres to have a sense of humor and incorporate it into your daily activities. Just keep things light. Resorting to humor about yourself and your situation can provide a number of benefits.

- *Raise hope.* According to research from Texas A&M University, humor may significantly raise your level of hope. And hope is what every small-business owner needs to face each new day.

- *Relieve stress.* A Canadian study from the University of Toronto showed that stressed-out people with a strong sense of humor were less anxious and depressed than stressed-out people without such a sense of humor.

- *Raise morale.* Who wants to work in a gloomy place?

- *Improve communication.* Interacting with your staff, suppliers, and the public is part of every day. Doing it with wit can spark greater responses. This doesn't mean using offensive jokes to bond with a new customer. It simply means adding a little fun and a smile to your engagements.

- *Accept change.* Change can be a difficult and stressful occurrence. But change happens all the time. Starting a business or moving to a new location is a dramatic change; switching from FedEx to United Parcel Service (UPS) or hiring a new employee is a minor change. Either way, don't view the change as the end of the world. Keep smiling.

- *Overcome mistakes.* Being able to laugh at yourself can help you put the past in perspective so you can move on.

LESSONS ABOUT ATTITUDE

✔ Orient yourself to be a business owner rather than an employee.

✔ Look at your company as a business rather than a hobby.

✔ Set goals you can attain.

✔ Write your goals by incorporating them into a business plan.

✔ Create a mission statement.

✔ Check your progress.

✔ Keep your sense of humor.

Delegate Effectively

Surround yourself with the best people you can find, delegate authority, and don't interfere as long as the policy you've decided upon is being carried out.

—Ronald Reagan

I f you are a freelance writer, consultant, or jewelry designer or are in some other solitary occupation, you may be able to handle every work responsibility by yourself, challenging and tiresome as this may be. But many small businesses, including sole proprietors, employ staff to do various activities. The Small Business Administration notes that in 2004 more than 5.5 million firms with fewer than 100 employees had a total more than 41 million people on their payrolls. In fact, small business is the job creation engine in our economy, responsible for 60 percent to 80 percent of new job creation.

There are good reasons for employing others to work with you—they'll share your load and may provide strength in areas in which you are weak. Most importantly, however, using employees frees you from routine tasks so you can do what you do best—run the company.

What types of workers can you use? You may, for example, employ a receptionist, administrative assistant, bookkeeper, salesperson, shipping clerk, or other employee on staff. An extra pair of hands can increase the earning capacity of your company. Or you may use outside workers—independent contractors or professionals—to help you with certain business activities.

In this chapter you will see the importance of working with others to handle, manage, and grow your business. You'll learn which type of worker—inside or outside—to use for what type of tasks and how to be an effective delegator. And you'll discover the special issues that arise when you work with family and friends.

Why to Delegate

Of course, no person you hire, no matter how much you pay or praise, will have the same passion and dedication to the business as you do. After all, you're the owner, so your business is your baby. But even knowing that anyone you take on will fall short of what you could do is no reason *not* to delegate. Delegation is a prerequisite to growing your business.

The term *delegation* usually is used in the context of a manager sharing responsibilities with those who are lower down the corporate ladder. However, we are using the term to apply to the small-business owner who shares the workload with others.

Shared Responsibilities

Even though the buck stops with you, it's helpful to share the load. The old adage that two heads are better than one applies to sharing responsibilities in your company. You gain another perspective on a job to be done.

It also means you don't have to be physically present during every hour your company is open. There's someone minding the store. Things can hum along even if you are on a sales call, visiting vendors, attending a trade show, or just taking time off.

Reducing Employee Turnover

Sharing responsibilities with employees can also lead to greater job satisfaction on their part because studies have shown that employees enjoy having greater responsibilities. Greater job satisfaction translates into more company loyalty and less employee turnover. According to the *Harvard Business Review*, an increase of just 5 percent in worker retention translates into a 10 percent drop in costs and a 25 percent to 65 percent increase in productivity.

And, believe it or not, one study shows that financial rewards—salary and benefits—are less of a factor in how employees view their jobs than emotional factors—job satisfaction and good relationships with others. In fact, the most common reasons that people leave their jobs include feeling they aren't appreciated, there is a lack of training and supervision, and there is insufficient opportunity for responsibility and growth. So delegating to employees means your employees are happier and your company can make more money.

Skills

You may be a people person who is terrible with numbers. You may be artistic but a complete idiot when it comes to computers. Or you may simply hate to call late-paying customers for collections. No matter how well you know your industry, you probably aren't adept at every aspect of running a business or may not like to do everything required in running a business. Here's where delegation comes in. You can share those tasks with someone who can handle them for you, often better than you can.

As your company grows, you can afford to take on more employees and increase specialization for each of your workers. For example, initially you may have one person handling all of your administrative chores. As your company gets larger and the workload increases, these administrative chores may be assigned among a receptionist, a secretary, and an assistant. That's what happened to a Web design company in New York City. The owner started it by himself but soon found a need to take on someone exclusively to do computer programming of the pages he designed. Then he hired a bookkeeper and another Web designer. Soon his business had expanded and relocated to larger facilities, needing a receptionist and more administrative staff.

Time

No matter how efficient you are, you can't add hours to the day. Delegating can shift time-consuming work to others so that you can concentrate on high-priority activities.

What to Delegate

Delegation means handing a task over to a subordinate. It doesn't mean abdicating your responsibility to see that things get done.

Appropriate Tasks to Delegate

The best type of activities to shift to others is routine tasks that eat up your time but certainly need to be done. If you could reduce the value of your time to an hourly rate, think of how costly it is for you to file your correspondence and how much better it would be for an hourly worker to do this for you.

Delegate activities in which you lack the skill or interest. Maybe you're not a people person and selling isn't your forte. Employing a salesperson to market your company's products or services can be a smart move. Delegate work to competent people who have the technical skills to handle their assignments.

What Not to Delegate

Don't delegate high-level decision-making authority. While anyone who assumes responsibility for a task should have some decision-making authority—whether to do something this way or that—it's up to you to make strategic decisions for your business. You can listen to suggestions—for example, whether to raise prices or expand into a new market—but ultimately you must decide whether to move ahead on the ideas.

Can you delegate decisions that involve spending money? For example, can you let your salesperson cut rates to a prospect in order to close a sale, even though the reduction costs you money? There's no fixed answer. Obviously, only you know your comfort zone when it comes to money matters. Are there dollar limits on decision making by others? Must all dollar decisions pass by your desk? Whatever you decide, be sure to clearly communicate the scope of authority you grant to others.

Whom to Delegate To

There are various ways to get the help you need to run your business. You can take on staff (in-house workers). You can use independent contractors, who are outside workers in business for themselves. Outside workers can be those plying the trade of your core business or outside professionals who are experts in their own fields. Or you can use temporary workers to meet certain needs.

Employees

Using employees is a long-term arrangement; when you hire someone, it is usually an indefinite commitment to keep that person on the payroll. One custom furniture maker who ran into hard times moonlighted as a short-order cook at a diner so he could keep his worker on staff and make payroll each week until his business improved. You may not have to go to such lengths, but you don't want to hire and fire with each upturn and downturn of your business.

Obviously, you want to hire and retain the best people you can. This is challenging for any company, but it can be particularly so for small businesses. You may not be able to offer the same benefits packages as large corporations. But you can offer something valued by employees: the opportunity to become involved in a business and take pride in their work. It often happens that employees in small businesses have greater responsibility for a wider range of areas than a comparable worker at a large corporation. This responsibility is usually appreciated; the employee gains experience in many areas and gains confidence in his or her abilities.

Employees need not be full-time or high-cost to your business. You can find people who will work the schedules you set, based on your company needs. For example, if you need some administrative help, a part-timer working 9 to 3 every day or 9 to 5 three days a week might be sufficient. Often you can find a highly qualified parent with school-age children or a semiretired individual to work the shorter hours you set.

Increasing your payroll can be a challenging decision for you. After all, when you take on someone new, you have made a financial commitment to that person and his or her family. They are depending on you. But in addition to financial considerations, a new person can change the dynamics of your workplace. No matter how small or how large, putting just one new person in the picture can alter longstanding work relationships. Recognizing this potential for change can help you ease the new person into your company.

Independent Contractors

Independent contractors (ICs) aren't necessarily contractors in the construction business; an IC can be any self-employed individual. Being self-employed means they have their own business.

Using ICs can be an effective way to gain the help you need without the management responsibilities that go along with employees. ICs work on their own, usually with little or no supervision on your part. Depending on their work assignment, they may work at a different location from you.

The challenge when using ICs is making sure the arrangement is clear. First, make sure both you and the IC understand that your relationship is *not* one of employer-employee. Rather, you are two business owners agreeing on work to be done by one party (the IC) for the benefit of another (that's you).

Go over all of the terms of the arrangement; preferably, put it in writing. This includes the work to be done, the deadline for completion, the amount and timing of payment for the work, and any other important details. For example, are you paying for the IC's travel time and costs? It is customary in independent contractor agreements to state that the IC understands that he or she is responsible for employment taxes.

Working with an IC, however, does not relieve you of the need for some supervision. You have to hold the IC accountable for the work and, depending on the nature of that work, check on progress at set points. Again depending on the type of work, this can be based on time (e.g., reviewing progress at the end of every week) or on the work itself (e.g., reviewing progress at predetermined points of a job).

Outside Professionals

These are accountants, lawyers, insurance agents, bankers, and other professionals. Using outside professionals is discussed in the next chapter.

Temporary Workers

If you have a special project that requires additional help, you don't have to beef up your payroll on a permanent basis. You may be able to use a temporary employment agency to meet your needs. For example, at year-end you may have additional book-keeping or accounting needs, such as preparing W-2 forms. If your staff is too busy for the extra work, a temporary worker skilled in whatever you need can fill the bill. For example, there's an accounting firm in southern California that uses a number of different temp workers during tax return preparation season to assist its 12 staff accountants. Some of the temps are accounting professionals, while others are clerical workers who assist in photocopying and assembling clients' returns.

The temporary worker is *not* your employee; he or she is the employee of the agency you contract with for the job. However, you retain the right to fire the worker at any time, so if the job isn't being done to your satisfaction, you can terminate the temporary worker and usually obtain a replacement from the agency.

While the temporary worker isn't your employee, you must still supervise the work being done. The temp usually works at your location using your equipment and following your rules. The extent of supervision required for a temp worker depends on the nature of the work and the level of experience the worker brings to the job.

You might also use an intern, who is usually a college student working for no pay to gain experience. The upside is the obvious cost savings; to the extent an intern can do the work you'd otherwise have to pay for, you save money. (And you may be creating a future employee because many companies decide to hire interns after graduation.) But the intern may require significant training and supervision, activities that can eat into your time and, thus, indirectly cost you money.

Choice of Worker

The choice of which type of worker to use—inside or outside—depends on many factors, including cost, industry practice, nature of the work, space and equipment, and IRS audit risk.

COST

On a straight dollar basis, it's more costly to put someone on the payroll than to use an independent contractor. For an employee, you are responsible for payroll taxes, which include the employer share of Social Security and Medicare taxes under the Federal Insurance Contribution Act (FICA), federal unemployment insurance under the Federal Unemployment Tax Act (FUTA), state unemployment insurance, and mandated workers' compensation and disability coverage. Also, if you have company benefit plans, such as a profit-sharing plan or health coverage, you usually must include employees and pay accordingly. As a rule of thumb, expect that the cost of each employee is about 1.25 to 1.4 times base salary after taking into account payroll taxes and benefits. Thus, for an employee earning a salary of $30,000, your total cost is more like $37,500 to $42,000; for an employee earning $75,000, your total cost can range from $93,750 to $105,000.

And besides ongoing compensation costs, there are usually high recruiting costs to find an employee through classified ads or job placement agencies—plus the cost of your time to review resumes and interview job candidates, and the cost for doing an employee background check. While recruiting costs can vary substantially with the type of job to be filled (it costs more to find higher-level employees), the U.S. Department of Labor conservatively estimates turnover cost at 33 percent of salary, or $10,000 for a $30,000 position. But many experts suggest that it may not be out of line to assume the cost at 100 percent to 150 percent of the salary, especially for higher-paid workers, so that it could cost $75,000 to $112,500 just to fill a $75,000 job.

INDUSTRY PRACTICE

What is customary in your type of business? For example, in construction, it is common practice to use independent tradespeople for a job; most small construction companies do not have a plumber or an electrician on the payroll.

NATURE OF THE WORK

The nature of the work you need done may, in some cases, suggest using an outside contractor. For example, you want to make design modifications to your web site or want to have someone maintain it for you. It may not make sense to put someone on the payroll for this limited project or amount of work. Web design and maintenance might not fill up a full day's work. An outside Web designer who bills you only for the time spent on your site may be a better choice.

SPACE AND EQUIPMENT

Do you have the room in your facilities to accommodate another person? If space is not a problem, then adding to your payroll may be the way to go. But if you work at home or are already over-crowded in your space and don't want to move to larger quarters, it may make sense to use an IC. You also have to provide equipment to employees to do their jobs. This may include at a minimum a computer and a telephone line. Make sure you can afford the equipment for a new employee. It is estimated that space and equipment costs add another 0.5 multiplier (50 percent) to base salary. So, for example, if an employee earns $30,000, it costs you an additional $15,000 annually. When added to the cost of employment taxes and benefits, the $30,000 compensation can jump to $52,500 to $57,000.

IRS AUDIT RISK

The IRS has said that reviewing worker classification as an employee or an independent contractor is one of its top priorities. The reason: More than $20 billion in employment taxes are at stake—it's easier to collect from an employer for several employees than to go after ICs one at a time. The main factor in deciding whether a worker is an employee or an IC is the question of control. If you can control the worker, dictating when, where, and how the work gets done, then the worker is your employee and you must treat him or her as such. This is so regardless of any labels you put on the arrangement or any contracts you might have with the workers.

How to Delegate

Delegating responsibility to see that certain things get done isn't a simple matter of telling someone to do it. Delegating is a multifaceted skill, involving recognition of what the worker should do, explaining how it should be done, supervising to see that it gets done when and how you want it to be done, and providing feedback to the worker that can lead to better performance in the future.

Job Description

When you see a task that needs to be done, you may instinctively know what to do. You don't write down the scope of the work; you just do it. But when you want someone else to do something, you must provide a complete description of the work to be done.

First explain the reason a job needs to be done. This helps your employee understand why the job (and the employee) is important to the company.

Then explain what needs to be done—the end goal of the project or task. You may need to break down the work into mini-jobs. Be clear about deadlines. You might want to create mini-deadlines for portions of a large project, just to be sure that things are on track.

Be clear about any constraints or limitations you want to include. For example, tell the employee whether overtime is barred or it is up to the discretion of the employee. Tell the employee whether or not he or she can involve other employees on the work.

Training

Just because you know how to create a great spreadsheet for a new sales project doesn't mean that your employee can also create one in keeping with your requirements.

Take the time up front to show your employee exactly what you want and how to do it. The time you put into training can be a time-saver—it eliminates the time needed to make corrections.

Employees usually are eager to take on more responsibility, but it may be best to dole it out in small pieces. Increase responsibility in increments to see that they can handle it.

Supervision

Some people are naturally self-starters who can jump in with both feet and tackle just about anything they face. Unfortunately, such people often start their own businesses and aren't working for someone else. But you can find competent employees who do not need hand-holding every step of the way. Your job is to see that the work progresses in a satisfactory manner. Don't micromanage every employee by controlling every detail in a meddlesome way. The owner of a small public relations firm in upstate New York hovered so much under the guise of being "helpful" that he continually drove competent employees away at lightning speed.

Devise a system for responsibly and efficiently overseeing all of your staff. Monitor each person's performance on a regular basis. This may be done, for example, by getting weekly reports—oral or written—from each person (larger companies may monitor departmental activities, but small-business owners may be more personally involved with each and every employee).

Monitoring someone's work doesn't mean spying (going through your employee's desk or listening in on phone calls). It means checking on the completion of work. If you set goals for a time period, you can see if they have been achieved.

Supervising doesn't mean solving everyone else's problems. Leave it to others to figure things out for themselves. Of course, you should be ready to offer any assistance or guidance when asked.

Use encouragement and praise to motivate employees to complete their assignments. You can't be an effective delegator if you are a perfectionist.

Recognize that despite your best efforts, not every employee you hire will work out. There may be a mismatch of personalities (something that can stand out in a small-business setting) or a failure of competence. Whatever the reason, don't let the problem continue indefinitely (it usually won't get better with time); terminate the employee and find a replacement.

Feedback

To help your employees grow in their jobs and enable them to take on ever-increasing responsibilities, you need to provide constructive criticism to them. Tell them what they did wrong (explaining why) and suggest how they can do better next time. Again, add praise to reinforce work done well. Also give tangible rewards for jobs well done, such as recognizing an employee of the month or giving a prized parking space for a valued employee.

Excuses for Not Delegating

It's easy to make excuses for not delegating work to others. You may even fool yourself into believing that you're doing the right thing for your business. Martyr complex? Like to be over-worked? Then this delusion may work for you. In truth, you should be delegating if the work level warrants it. Here are some common excuses for not delegating, and good reasons why the excuses are lame.

- "No one can do it as well as I can." You may be correct; you may do things better. But you can't do it all, so you should decide what you can delegate and get on with it. Recognize that it's going to take someone longer to do something than it takes you—at least until the person becomes familiar with the work. Their competency will grow in no time.

- "I'm a perfectionist." If you want every detail of every job just so and believe only you can accomplish this, you may be doomed to stay small. At the very least, you're certain to become exhausted!

- "I enjoy getting my hands dirty." Some owners of growing businesses like to stay in the game, remembering when things were very small and they could go it alone. They have difficulty making a transition to the new role of owner-overseer. But if they fail to make this transition, business growth won't be sustained.

- "I don't have the time to train or supervise." The time you put in up front can produce greater free time for you later on.

- "I don't like losing control." If you're a control freak, your business may be doomed to stay small and not expand. You have to be willing to give up *some* control in order to gain company growth.

Special Concerns for Family Businesses

According to the MassMutual Financial Group/Raymond Institute American Family Business Survey done in 2002, there are more than 24 million family-owned businesses in the United States. In these companies controlled by family members many employees are related by blood or marriage and include spouses, children, parents, cousins, or other relatives. Some small-business owners also hire their friends.

Nepotism—the policy of giving consideration based on familial relationship rather than on merit—generally has a bad connotation. But working with those you are connected with has many advantages. There can be a level of trust that is difficult to achieve with outsiders. And, often, hiring younger family members is a way to train the next generation to take over the business. The owner of a small art supply store in the New York metropolitan area put his two young boys to work, teaching them the ropes. These boys grew up to eventually take over and expand the company into a multistate business doing more than $35 million in sales and are grooming their own children for management roles in the future.

As challenging as it may be to delegate to unrelated employees, the job becomes even trickier when it comes to a family member or friend. Family dynamics can play a role when you have to supervise someone close to you, especially a parent. The role reversal that results can create difficult feelings. And, of course, when problems arise, it can be emotionally more difficult to fire a relative or friend if you want to preserve the personal relationship.

To avoid problems when working with those who are close to you, make sure to discuss your concerns at the start of the arrangement. Try to anticipate potential problems, such as jealousy that may arise among nonrelated employees. Be clear about the job you want your relative to do. You don't want your uncle assuming he has the authority to make decisions you reserve for yourself. But you do want your uncle to have sufficient authority to do his job properly. Giving authority creates respect that usually becomes mutual. And it's a good idea to pay your relative no more—and no less—than you would any other employee for the work to be done.

LESSONS ABOUT DELEGATING

✔ Delegate if you want to grow your business.

✔ Decide to whom you are going to delegate work.

✔ Create procedures to follow for effective delegation.

✔ Overcome excuses that are preventing you from delegating.

✔ Use special care when working with family and/or friends.

Turn to Experts

Experts should be on tap, not on top.

—Sir Winston Churchill

*O*wning a business means having to deal with many things no one person collecting a paycheck ever has to. You have to see to it that your company keeps good financial records, complies with the law, has sufficient insurance coverage for all contingencies, and has the cash to pay your bills—which are all separate tasks from providing the goods and services that define your company. Can you do all of this on your own? Probably not. You may not know, for example, what laws you are required to meet. Here's where the help of experts comes in.

Experts can provide guidance on an as-needed basis to fill in the gaps in your knowledge and abilities. They don't take your place. They don't relieve you of your responsibilities to see to all of these activities. You're the quarterback to your team of experts.

In this chapter you will see which types of experts can help you in your business and how to find them. You will also learn about resources you can turn to for assistance that will cost you little or nothing. And you will also find out how to establish and use a board of advisers to help you develop and implement sound business goals.

Stable of Experts

You can't be an expert in everything unless you want to be a jack-of-all-trades and a master of none. In running your business you need to turn to a variety of professionals who can counsel you on a wide range of topics, including legal matters, accounting issues, insurance, technology, and more.

Large corporations usually have experts on the payroll to provide ongoing help in their areas of expertise. There may be an in-house counsel providing legal advice, a chief financial officer (CFO) providing accounting and money direction, and an information technology (IT) manager to monitor computers and so forth. Small businesses usually hire outside professionals to meet these requirements on an as-needed basis.

Small-business owners are unusually self-reliant and often like to find answers for themselves and do things on their own. This attribute may be great when it comes to making decisions about a product or service or how to handle a customer problem; it can be dangerous when problems arise in areas in which they lack expertise. For example, do you know whether you are complying with new federal overtime rules? Do you carry the right type of insurance coverage for optimum protection? These are the types of questions that experts can help you with.

It is a good idea to develop relationships with experts you can turn to when issues arise and you need help. Include in your contact list at least one of each of the following experts:

- An attorney

- An accountant

- A banker

- An insurance agent or broker

- An IT consultant

Try to develop an association with each of these professionals, even if you do not have any immediate or pressing need for their services now. This will enable you to call upon them when problems arise and you need prompt assistance.

Your Attorney

You may need to use an attorney from time to time. For most small businesses, legal advice and assistance is not needed on a regular basis. Rather, you use an attorney for specific issues that you may face in the life of your business—from start-up to your exit strategy. It's a good idea to use an attorney to:

- *Set up your company's legal framework.* For example, an attorney can advise you on whether to incorporate your business or form a limited liability company. The attorney can also perform the necessary steps to get you going, such as incorporating your business and setting up your corporate bylaws and minutes. It may be possible for you to do some things yourself, but it may not be the best course of action. The few dollars you spend one time on legal fees for incorporating, for example, are well worth it. The owner of a very profitable horse farm in upstate New York tried to do everything herself, including electing S corporation status for her newly incorporated farm. Unfortunately, she filed the federal election but failed to file the required New York election form. The result: She owed state franchise taxes that would otherwise have been avoided had she simply paid an attorney to complete her incorporation and make her S elections.

- *Protect your intellectual property.* Do you have a logo? A slogan? It may be worth it to register for trademark protection with the U.S. Patent and Trademark Office (USPTO at www.uspto.gov). The process is complex and you should use an expert to assist you.

- *Review your leases and contracts.* Before you sign anything—a lease, a contract, or any agreement—have it reviewed by an attorney. This applies to commercial loan agreements as well. Don't bind yourself to terms you can't live with.

- *Advise you on succession planning.* What happens to your business if you retire? Die? If you have co-owners it is a good idea to have a buy-sell agreement to protect you interests in case you or any co-owner wants out for any reason or dies. An attorney can explain your buy-sell options and draft an appropriate agreement.

■ *Structure the sale of the business.* If you are selling your interest, in whole or in part, you want an attorney to advise you on the best way to accomplish your goals and see to it that your intentions are translated into legally binding agreements.

Finding an Attorney

Like your personal doctor, you may want to locate an attorney through a referral from someone you know and trust. For instance, you can ask your banker, your accountant, or a friend or relative for a referral to an attorney.

RESOURCES

If you cannot find the right referral—say you need an attorney specializing in intellectual property but your brother knows only a good corporate attorney—consider using the following resources to find a referral:

● American Bar Association (ABA) (www.abanet.org, click on "Lawyer Locator" to access the Martindale.com resource).

● Attorney Find (www.attorneyfind.com); search by state and category of law.

● Legal Guru (www.legalguru.com, click on "Find Attorneys"); search by area of law and your state.

● Lexis-Nexis (www.lawyers.com, click on "Business Users"); enter the type of lawyer you are looking for.

● Martindale.com (www.martindale.com, click on "Lawyer Locator" and then "Location/Area of Practice"). This resource is by far the most comprehensive (it is the same one you'll find through the ABA).

● Respond.com (www.respond.com, click on "Legal" and then on the area of practice in which you need help).

Cost

It is customary to pay an attorney an hourly rate for services provided. Attorneys' fees vary widely, depending on location and expertise. For example, in New York City some attorneys charge in excess of $600 per hour for a partner's services in a large law firm, but in other places you may pay under $100 per hour. Rates are usually lower for associate attorneys and paralegals. In some cases, you may pay a flat rate for a specific job (e.g., $500 for incorporation services). Or you may pay a contingency fee, which is a percentage of a recovery (e.g., 40 percent for collecting money that is owed to you).

Before you engage an attorney, you should be provided with a retainer agreement or letter of explanation detailing billing rates and other terms. Make sure you understand these terms. For example, you may be billed for extras, such as photocopying, faxing, and postage.

Online Resources for Legal Advice

If you don't want or can't afford to pay an attorney to answer day-to-day questions that may arise, you may be able to find the answers you need through various online resources. For example, you want to be sure that the questions to ask when interviewing perspective employees do not violate nondiscrimination laws or whether you can do a background check on someone you want to hire.

RESOURCES

Check a specific question rather than using a lawyer to handle a legal matter at these resources:

- FreeAdvice (http://freeadvice.com) lets you search over 600,000 answers to questions.

- LawGuru.com (www.lawguru.com) contains the largest free database of legal questions and answers. There are also legal forms you can download (but have your own attorney review them before you use them).

Your Accountant

The IRS says that 80 percent of small businesses use outside accountants. There is a good reason for using this type of expert. The tax laws—federal, state, and local—are constantly changing. The business tax rules you learned this year may not serve you for the coming year. You need someone knowledgeable in the latest rules to help you take advantage of every opportunity in the tax law to save money. You also need an accountant to make sure you do not overlook any tax responsibilities so you stay out of trouble and avoid costly penalties. An accountant can also audit your books and check that tax returns have been filed in a timely fashion. And, perhaps most importantly, you want someone who can advise you on your business practices. For example, a good accountant can help you with inventory management to cut costs or advise when to change your method of accounting to create income or loss as needed. One retailer's accountant was tracking the company's sales and was able to detect problems even though revenues weren't immediately affected.

Don't, however, expect that an accountant will give you some secret formula or strategy for beating the IRS. If he or she does suggest some supposedly unknown method, you probably want to steer clear of this person, who may lead you into trouble, and find a reputable adviser.

Caution: Be advised that most information you impart to your accountant, unlike information you tell your attorney, is *not* privileged, and your accountant can be compelled to divulge it in a lawsuit or to a government agency under certain circumstances. The only communications to your accountant that are protected are those in noncriminal federal tax matters (some states provide similar protection for state tax matters). But anything you say before a third party or having to do with criminal federal matters or before a federal agency other than the IRS, such as the Securities and Exchange Commission (SEC), is not privileged.

Finding an Accountant

Obviously the best way to find an accountant, as in the case of an attorney, is through a referral from someone you trust. If you already have an attorney, ask him or her for a referral.

RESOURCES

To obtain a referral to an accountant, go to:

- American Institute of Certified Public Accountants (AICPA) at www.aicpa.org/yellow/ypascpa.htm for links to state societies of CPAs. You can contact your state society for local referrals.

- National Association of Tax Professionals (www.tax professionals.com and click on "Find a Professional Near You").

- National Society of Accountants (www.nsacct.org and click on "Find a Professional").

Note: For your business, you probably want to rely on a certified public accountant (CPA), someone who has passed the licensing requirements of the American Institute of Certified Public Accountants. But, depending on the situation, you may find the help you need with a regular public accountant—someone with an accounting degree but who does not have CPA designation.

Cost

The fees you pay to an accountant depend on the work to be done. Your accountant may handle your payroll and income tax returns. Or you may do this in-house and turn to an accountant only for specific questions that arise.

The accountant may quote you a fixed payment for a set amount of work (e.g., $1,000 for your business tax return). Or you may pay an hourly rate for services. Hourly rates for accountants vary considerably nationwide from under $100 per hour to several hundred dollars per hour.

Your Banker

Mark Twain noted that "a banker is a fellow who lends you his umbrella when the sun is shining but wants it back the minute it begins to rain." Develop a relationship with your banker when the sun is shining so you may be able to use his umbrella when it rains.

Today many banks, large and small, are courting small businesses with expanded banking hours, free checking, and other business services. But when it comes to lending money, these banks may not be any more friendly now than in the past. It's not easy for small businesses to borrow money, even though it may be vital to their survival.

Lack of sufficient capital is the number one reason why businesses fail. So create a banking relationship you can depend on when you need additional funds. Be sure to pick the right bank; it may not necessarily be the one with the lowest checking fees or longest banking hours. You want to find a bank that has the most liberal lending policies. And you want to make the correct choice as early as you can—even before you start the business. Here's why.

Say you have borrowed $75,000 from Bank A. Your business is expanding and now you want a $50,000 business line of credit as well. But under Bank A's lending criteria you qualify for only $75,000. You find out that under Bank B's lending criteria you could qualify for a $125,000 loan. However, Bank B will not make the $125,000 loan until you've paid off the $75,000 outstanding loan. This may force you to use your own money (if you have it) to pay off the old loan just to obtain the new one.

If you are a start-up (in banking terms this usually means a business in its first three years of existence), make sure to find a bank that makes start-up loans; not all banks do.

Also determine whether the bank participates in Small Business Administration (SBA) loan programs. The SBA does not make loans; it guarantees loans to small businesses as a way to encourage commercial lenders to make the loans. SBA loans may have favorable application processes and loan terms, so find out up front whether they are available through a bank you are considering.

Finding a Banker

You want a bank that makes small-business loans; some banks are more aggressive than others in this type of financing. Ask a prospective banker how many small-business loans have been made in the past 12 months to discern the bank's attitude toward small-business lending. You also want to establish a personal relationship so that the banker views you as a partner and won't call your loan at the first sign of financial trouble.

Start with the bank at which you maintain your personal account. As an existing customer you may qualify for more favorable terms on a business account. But the branch manager, the person who may greet you at the door, usually is not the person with whom to create a business banking relationship. The manager, who can help you on administrative matters on your business bank account, may be able to steer you to the bank's small-business lending officer. This person is the gatekeeper for all your financing needs.

Interview the small-business lending officer as you would anyone who works for you. Make sure you can develop rapport. Be prepared to present in-depth information about your business (e.g., a formal business plan or at least various financial statements) so the banker can tell you whether your company can meet the bank's lending criteria and so you can decide whether to establish a relationship.

Your Insurance Agent

According to the National Federation of Independent Business (NFIB), being sued is one of the biggest fears of small-business owners. And there's good reason for this fear: Even fighting frivolous lawsuits that you ultimately win can cost thousands of dollars. Even worse, losing a lawsuit can wreak financial and emotional hardship on you, taking you years to rebuild and recoup your loss. The best defense against lawsuits is adequate insurance coverage so the insurance company must defend you if you are sued and will pay any damages that may result (up to the limits of the policy). Because of the importance of having the right coverage, it is essential to have a good insurance agent.

An insurance agent can advise you on the type of coverage you should carry. For example, do you now have employment practices liability insurance (EPLI)? This type of coverage protects you from claims of employees such as age discrimination, sexual harassment, and wrongful termination. Many small-business owners may not even know such coverage exists or think they need it.

Which type of insurance professional do you need? An insurance *agent* sells insurance for one company (e.g., The Hartford). An insurance *broker* sells products for more than one company. Insurance professionals do not charge you for their services; they are compensated from the insurance company by means of commissions on the insurance products you purchase.

Finding an Insurance Agent

As with any other professional, referrals are the best way to find an insurance expert. However, if you cannot find one that sells the type of coverage you think you need, you can contact the insurance company directly to receive a referral for someone in your area. For example, say you think you need directors and officers (D&O) insurance (for protection when someone sues the company). Contact insurance companies selling this type of coverage (such as AIG Small Business and Chubb).

Your Information Technology Consultant

Technology is changing so fast that it's practically impossible to keep up with developments. Yesterday's pagers have given way to cell phones. Dial-up modems have been replaced first by broadband and mobile technology. Surely your business needs to use technology, to a greater or lesser extent, in its daily operations—to track expenses, sell through e-commerce, stay in touch with customers, communicate with vendors, and access information vital to your company. How can you stay up-to-date on the technology that can be used to run your business better and for less cost? You may want to rely on an information technology (IT) expert. Most small businesses cannot afford to have a full-time in-house employee managing IT issues and must use outside consultants for this purpose.

Role of Your IT Consultant

You probably need twofold assistance for your small business. First, you need someone who can help you manage your current technology to keep you humming. When your computers are down, you may be virtually out of business.

Second, you want someone who can guide you to new technology so you can stay ahead of the curve. The consultant can explain what the newest development is all about and whether it is advisable for you to get it.

Finding an IT Consultant

As with other experts, IT consultants typically advertise their services in the usual venues—yellow pages and on the Web. You might also find a good referral to a local consultant from your nearest computer store. There are some regional and national databases to help you search for a consultant in your area. For example, the Professional and Technical Consultants Association (www.patca.org) has an online database that you can search by area of expertise, city, members (alphabetically), company, or member profile by keyword.

It may not be easy for you to assess an IT consultant's qualifications, especially when you may not fully understand exactly what they do. Certification can help. Look for consultants who have some official certification from vendors such as Microsoft, IBM, Sun Microsystems, and QuickBooks. Check for membership in a recognized professional organization for IT consultants, such as the Association for Computing Machinery (ACM) or the Institute of Electrical and Electronics Engineers (IEEE). Make sure the person you interview understands what you want done and then leave it to the expert to decide how this gets done. As you would do with filling any employee position, it usually is wise to interview at least two or three consultants before making a selection.

Cost

What you'll pay for IT services depends on your location, what you want the consultant to do, and his or her level of experience.

There is no easy generalization. You may pay a fixed monthly rate for your computer maintenance services. You may pay an hourly rate when you call the consultant in for a specific project or problem. It is not untypical to pay between $600 and $1,200 for a full day of consulting.

Your best practice is to understand clearly what you want the consultant to do and how he or she will be compensated. Put your agreement in writing.

Other Consultants

The types of experts discussed throughout this chapter may not be the only ones you need. You may want to engage specialists in marketing, public relations, Web design, import-export documentation, or industry-specific needs. For example, if you use machinery in your business, you may need expert advice on the latest technology to upgrade your systems and stay competitive.

Whenever you engage a consultant or expert, make sure you fully understand the terms of the arrangement. What do you expect the expert to do for you? What will it cost you? What is your redress if you are not satisfied with the services you received? This may sound like commonsense advice, but it is all too easy to forget when you are pressed with a problem and want immediate help from an expert.

Expert Resources

You don't necessarily need an expert on retainer to get the help and guidance you are seeking for every problem or question you face. You might find useful information and assistance from a variety of resources. This type of help may be most useful when you have a particular question that you can articulate (rather than vague misgivings about a certain practice or activity of your business). It may cost you little or nothing to check out these resources before you go to your own stable of experts. You can then pass these ideas across your expert's desk for further consideration.

RESOURCES

Find expert advice and guidance at:

- Business Owners' IdeaCafe (www.businessownersideacafe .com) provides tips and ideas from experts on e-commerce, marketing, and managing your business.

- Entrepreneur.com (www.entrepreneur.com), an online off-shoot of *Entrepreneur* magazine, offers not only articles on a wide range of topics, but also the opportunity to connect to business coaches in areas such as business plans, guerrilla marketing, and raising money. You can view the experts' bios and submit your questions to them by e-mail.

- Jim Blasingame: The Small Business Advocate (www .smallbusinessadvocate.com) has a wealth of information on many topics of interest to you. Listen to archived radio shows with experts in all fields. Read online articles from "The Brain Trust," comprised of dozens of top experts in more than three dozen subjects, such as franchising, technology, and importing and exporting.

- SCORE, Counselors to America's Small Business (www.score.org), is a national nonprofit organization that provides free, personalized counseling offered by a group of volunteers who work closely with the Small Business Administration (SBA). SCORE counselors can help you with such areas as marketing strategies, business plans, and commercial financing options. You can also e-mail questions (there are 1,200 e-mail counselors) and receive answers within 48 hours.

- Small business development centers (SBDCs) (www .sba.gov/sbdc), which are administered by the SBA, deliver up-to-date, confidential counseling, training, and technical assistance in all aspects of small business management.

(Continued)

RESOURCES *(Continued)*

- Smallbiz Advice (www.smallbizadvice.com) connects you to experts who can assist you in whatever area you need help in. The referral is free (you simply register at the site), but you pay for the services you receive from the expert you select. The fee may be lower than you would otherwise pay for the help; it is arranged on an auction basis.

- State economic development agencies and their local offices can steer you to the help you need and provide technical assistance to you.

Caution: There are a lot of bloggers online offering small-business advice. While their thoughts may be interesting and sound authoritative, use care in relying on the opinion of bloggers. Their suggestions may be based solely on their opinions and sometimes may even give you misinformation.

Board of Advisers

Big corporations use a board of directors to review and approve the strategic direction of the business and to monitor the activities of the company. By law, a corporate board is responsible for the affairs of the corporation and is responsible to shareholders. More specifically, a board of directors usually:

- Approves the annual budget.
- Authorizes executive compensation, including bonuses.
- Adopts fringe benefit plans, such as qualified retirement plans and medical reimbursement plans.
- Meets legal requirements to hold meetings and take other actions.

But most small companies do not use boards of directors. First of all, small companies may not be corporations, so directors are not mandatory. Second, small companies usually cannot afford to compensate expert outside directors.

But small businesses can and should use a board of advisers. Unlike a board of directors, there is no legal authority invested in a board of advisers; they can give advice, but it isn't binding on you to accept it. The reasons for having a board of advisers include:

- It is very helpful if your company wants a commercial loan, since a banker may look more favorably on a small business that has the guidance of experts (this information is usually included in a business plan submitted as part of a loan application).

- If your company is a family business, having a board of advisers can alleviate tensions and provide impartial opinions on what should be done.

There are two ways to get the board you need: Create your own board by pulling together knowledgeable businesspeople who can contribute their expertise and advice on your behalf, or use prefab boards put together for you by independent companies or family business centers at universities that provide this service.

Create Your Own Board

You may already be working with several very qualified experts, each of whom is giving you advice. But the advice you receive may be one-sided. For example, maybe your accountant is suggesting you do something from a financial viewpoint that your lawyer would tell you is not advisable from a legal perspective. By having an accountant and an attorney sit down together and discuss the issue, you may arrive at a new and probably better-informed decision.

Your board can work in much the same way as a focus group to react to new ideas and help develop strategies from these ideas. Or use your board like a think tank to generate new ideas rather than simply react to yours.

Your board should consist of an accountant, a financial adviser, a legal expert, and a marketing professional. Your board may also include a human resources (HR) person. The accountant you have on your board may or may not be your company accountant. You may prefer independent advisers to those who are already acting as your consultants. You want enough members to provide a diversity of opinion, but you don't want so many that the meetings become unwieldy. Make sure the members you select are a good fit and that personalities won't get in the way of helping your business.

Use a Prefab Board

Don't know the right experts to call upon for your board of advisers? Then use the help of a company or family business center that can create your board for you.

There are several companies that provide this assistance for a fee. They bring together business leaders from like-sized (noncompeting) companies who work with small-business owners to provide practical advice and guidance. Usually, these leaders run their own companies in different business sectors, including business services, construction, distribution, manufacturing, personal services, and retail. The owner of a tuxedo rental company in Minneapolis used just such an advisory board to gain insight in such unfamiliar areas as market development, strategic planning, and financial management. If your company is family-owned, you might turn to a family business center at a university; the center usually helps you put a board together.

RESOURCES

To find help in setting up a board of advisers, go to:

• Economic development programs found at many universities nationwide. For example, the Small Business Advisory Board Council is an economic development program that operates within the University of Central Florida Small Business Development Center (www.advisoryboard council.org and click on "About the Council") and is significantly funded by Orange County's economic stimulus package. The Council acts as a matchmaker between central Florida businesses and volunteer advisers, at no cost to you.

- Family business centers nationwide, often on college campuses such as the University of Massachusetts and the University of Wisconsin—Madison, can help you with all aspects of an advisory board. To find a family business center near you, just do an online search for "family business centers."

- *Family Business* magazine online directory of advisers, which includes family business centers, professional firms, and financial institutions serving family businesses around the world, lets you search at www.familybusinessmagazine.com (click on "Adviser Directory") or http://library.family businessmagazine.com/directory/default.shtml for what you need by location and category.

- TAB (The Alternative Board) at www.tabboards.com is a private company that provides facilitators trained in running these board meetings so there is active participation by members that results in constructive advice to you.

- TEC: Chief Executives Working Together at www.teconline .com works with small-business owners to form a board of advisers.

How to Make Your Board Work Effectively

Just having a board of advisers doesn't automatically guarantee you are better off than if you had no board. You have to work with the board in a smart way to get something out of the arrangement. Here are some tips for making your board work for you:

- *Define the role of the board.* Unlike a board of directors, whose role is dictated by law, your board of advisers' role is what you say it is. You can involve them in as much minutia as you want or use them only as a steering committee for your ideas. In defining the role of the board, think of it as if you are providing a job description—detail what you want a member to do for your business.

- *Schedule meetings.* How often should your board meet? There's no fixed answer. It depends on how much you need their guidance for day-to-day operations, members' availability, and what you can afford (you pay for their time as explained in the next subsection). Once or twice a month may be ideal. If meetings stretch to quarterly, they may not prove to be of much value because too much can happen in the interim.

- *Communicate with board members.* From notification of meetings to developments in your company and industry, you have to keep board members well informed. If you don't honestly share your problems, you won't get the help you need.

- *Set the agenda.* It's up to you to lay out what areas of concern you want the board to focus on. Include such topics as your company finances, marketing strategies, new products or services on the horizon, or a proposed relocation.

- *Give adequate notice.* Your board members need time to fit the meeting in their schedules and to prepare for the upcoming meeting. Even if you have a fixed date (e.g., at 4:00 P.M. on the last Monday of every month), reminders are helpful. Advise board members of the meeting by mail or e-mail. Mark the envelope or subject line of the e-mail as "Board Meeting Notice" so it is not overlooked. It wouldn't hurt to personally phone each member the day before the meeting as a final reminder.

- *Run the meeting tightly.* An advisory board meeting isn't the forum for socializing and casual conversation. Keep to the agenda set for the meeting. Limit discussion on agenda items as needed to fit the meeting within the time allotted.

Cost

It is customary to pay board members for their participation (unless you are using volunteer advisers). Board members aren't company employees; they are independent contractors paid for their services.

There is no set rate you must pay board members. You can negotiate with your board. However, in addition to reimbursement for travel expenses, it is usual to pay $500 or more per member per meeting. Compensation to members is important to ensure you have quality advisers.

It is also a good idea to carry directors and officers (D&O) insurance (even though your board has only advisers and not directors). This type of coverage protects directors/advisers and officers from personal liability if the company is sued. The cost of such insurance varies with the level of coverage (e.g., $1 million, $5 million, $10 million coverage). Usually, an adviser wants to see a letter of indemnification from the company agreeing to accept legal responsibility for his or her actions in the capacity of an adviser.

LESSONS ABOUT USING EXPERTS

✔ Create a stable of experts you can turn to for advice.

✔ Find experts on whom you can rely through referrals and other resources.

✔ Use resources that can cost you little or no money to tap into experts on a wide range of subjects.

✔ Use a board of advisers to help obtain guidance in running your business.

Manage Your Time

Time is money.

—Benjamin Franklin

*I*f you're like other small-business owners, you work long hours. Small-business owners work on average 52 hours a week (according to a 2000 survey by New York marketing firm Willard & Shullman), compared with the average employee, who works 34.2 hours a week (U.S. Bureau of Labor Statistics). Still, even with all these hours there just doesn't seem to be enough time to do everything that needs to be done.

You can't add to the hours in a day, but you can learn to manage your time better in order to maximize the use of those hours. You can learn to schedule your time more effectively, delegate activities to others to free up your time, and take other steps to make the most of every day. Of course, many suggestions for managing your time may seem like common sense, but they can easily be overlooked or forgotten in your hectic day-to-day routine.

In this chapter you will learn about the importance of time management. You'll see how scheduling and delegating can add to your productivity. You can find out which time-saving devices can be used to better manage your time. You'll learn how to clean out clutter to make it easier to find things, not only saving you time but also helping you avoid frustration. Most importantly, you'll learn how to say no so that you don't get bogged down in time-consuming activities you shouldn't be involved in.

Importance of Time Management

Before electricity, for the most part work hours were limited by daylight and weather conditions. If you worked outside and the weather was inclement, you stayed home. When your candle burned down, you went to bed. But now work can be done 24/7. So it's up to you to decide when and how long to work and what to work on.

There are several reasons why is managing your time so important. First, time is finite; you only have so much time in which to fit your activities each day. The Roman poet Horace said, "Carpe diem! . . . (Seize the day, put no trust in the morrow!)" Make the most of what you have. It is later than you think. Second, time is fleeting; it passes and you can miss out on opportunities if you don't jump on them when you have the chance. According to a Danish proverb, "Time waits for no man" (or woman), so you have to seize opportunities when they present themselves and make sure that time, and opportunities, do not pass you by. Third, time mismanagement can create problems for you and your business. If mismanagement is serious enough, it can be your undoing.

One of the key problems that small-business owners face from time mismanagement is burnout. *Merriam-Webster's Collegiate Dictionary* defines this as "exhaustion of physical or emotional strength or motivation usually as a result of prolonged stress or frustration." The term may have first come to be used in connection with social workers who faced overwhelming caseloads that couldn't be managed in the time they had. They had glazed eyes and even became insensitive to the job that needed to be done. Today, burnout can affect anyone, including the small-business owner, and it can result from having too much to do and too little time to do it.

Burnout can produce both psychological and physical symptoms, including fatigue, irritability, forgetfulness, lack of concentration, and low productivity. It can even lead to serious health problems, such as depression, illness, and addictions. For the small-business owner, burnout in the extreme may bring the demise of your company—if you can't work up to your full potential, or perhaps can't work at all, your business may not be able to survive. How can you help prevent burnout?

- Don't feel that you must work 16 hours a day, every day, just so your business can make it. Set limits on your work schedule so that you don't burn the midnight oil each and every day. Make sure to take at least one day off each week, no matter what.

- Learn to better manage your time so you make sure important things are attended to and you continue to enjoy your business.

Learn to Schedule Your Time

In order to schedule effectively, first determine your style of handling your daily activities. We are all different, whether you label some type A or morning people versus type B or slower starters. Personality and/or style dictate the type of scheduling that may work best.

Some business owners prefer to prioritize, tackling the most important jobs first and leaving the administrative tasks for the end of the day. Others like to clear their desks of the trivial jobs that can be distracting; by disposing of them first, they can devote their full attention to the big things. There's no right or wrong way; whatever works for you is the method to select and follow.

If you're a day person, you may want to handle key matters when you're still fresh, while a night person would be better off approaching such things gradually. Or consider scheduling only your important tasks and filling in your odd (unscheduled) moments with trivial jobs or things that can be done quickly.

If you work at home, regularly or occasionally, you can integrate your personal responsibilities with your business activities. A nurse in Arizona who stayed home to care for her child started an eBay business that grew into a full-time endeavor. Her "full-time," however, was largely after 11 at night into the wee hours of the morning when her child was asleep. Whatever hours you choose to work, you need to follow the same tips for effective time management.

Note It Down

This may seem like the most obvious suggestion, but if you don't keep a record of appointments, project deadlines, and other things you have to do for easy reference, you might just forget to do them, and trying to remember each one can distract you from other issues. Of course, keeping track of things doesn't necessarily mean jotting things down. You can use a voice recorder to make note of ideas, and personal digital assistants (PDAs) or similar devices to track your appointments. The point is to not keep track of things merely in your head.

Include on your list not only your major ongoing projects, but also mundane clerical or ministerial activities that need to be done. Don't fail to schedule time, for example, to meet with your accountant on a regular basis. Be sure to keep in touch with customers you haven't worked with in some time. Make your to-do list a part of your daily calendar—on your Day-Timer or other day planner or with software or online solutions, as discussed later in this section.

Plot Out Time Blocks

Instead of jumping from a sales call to strategic planning to answering e-mail, it's better to set aside blocks of time to dispose of similar tasks. For example, set aside one hour at the start of the day to read and answer e-mail and organize or review your daily calendar. One hour at the end of the day can be devoted to returning phone calls and answering correspondence. Find out what time blocks work best for you, given both your personality/style and the industry you are in.

Of course, you need to remain flexible. As a small-business owner you're well aware that the unexpected *always* happens. Just when you're about to return a phone call, a crisis can erupt that needs your immediate attention. Make sure your scheduling has enough room to accommodate the daily emergencies that are bound to arise.

Prioritize Your Activities

If you can do only one thing in the time you've allotted, what would it be? Probably something that's important or time sensitive rather than something that is trivial or can wait.

Some people find that a grading system—assigning importance to a task from 1 to 5 or A through E—helps to keep priorities straight. It doesn't mean that a trivial matter assigned a 5 won't get done; it only means that it must wait until you've completed your 1 through 4 tasks.

Use New Scheduling Tools

Technology can help you draw up a schedule and stick to it. For many people, a paper calendar is a thing of the past. And many small-business owners cannot afford a secretary or personal assistant to remind them of appointments and other commitments. So the old scheduling tools have been replaced by PDAs, such as Palms, Black-Berrys, or other handheld devices, or desktop computer calendars for automating scheduling. Using technology makes sense because it saves you time and is often a great convenience.

RESOURCES

Here are some examples of technological aids (some of which offer a free 30-day trial option) that you can use to help you organize your day and remember what you have to do:

- Calendarscope from Duality Software ($29.95 to purchase the product) is a calendar and software-scheduling program that can be used with your computer and synchronized with Palm OS. It includes reminder alarms and enables users to schedule daily, weekly, and monthly events (www.calendarscope.com).

- Microsoft bCentral Appointment Manager ($29.95 monthly for the standard version, or $99 a month for the professional version) lets you manage appointments and schedules online (www.bcentral.com/products/am/default.asp).

- Microsoft Outlook 2003 ($109 for this separate software; can be purchased as part of Microsoft Office 2003) is a comprehensive software program for organizing and managing appointments and other tasks. You may already have this software loaded on your computer and not realize it (www.microsoft.com).

Learn to Delegate

You can't do it all by yourself. You need to let others handle the jobs they can do on their own and keep yourself free to concentrate on important matters. Let employees deal with clerical tasks. If you're a one-person operation, outsource some of the work you've been doing and give yourself more time to devote to other things.

Delegating is a skill that involves learning how to get employees and outside contractors to handle tasks you've been doing up to now. But delegating starts with a decision to turn over responsibility to someone else. This isn't easy for many small-business owners to do. How to delegate effectively is discussed in Chapter 2; using outside experts not only for advice but also to free up your time is discussed in Chapter 3.

Overcome Procrastination

Procrastination—putting off doing something until later that you know should be done now—can wreak havoc with the best-laid time-management plans. It can result in your missing opportunities or having to face frenzied last-minute deadlines and can kill your sense of joy at work. Of course, everyone procrastinates sometimes, especially when facing an unpleasant, difficult, or confusing task. For example, if you hate to make cold calls, you can probably find a million excuses and other things to do that prevent you from cold calling. But effective time management requires that you overcome your inclination to procrastinate.

Change Your Attitude

You can get to what you have to do and avoid procrastination if you change your thinking. Get rid of unreal expectations that can prevent you from starting a project. For example, you don't always have to be a perfectionist; just make up your mind to do the best job you can in the time you have. Don't be put off from starting a task just because you won't be able to finish it—make a start and schedule more time later on. Breaking down a job into smaller parts makes it more manageable and less daunting. Realize that if the work that you're facing is unpleasant, boring, or distasteful, it isn't a fine wine and won't get any better with age. You may hate making collections calls to late-paying customers, but you might as well get it over with because the calls can't be avoided, and waiting won't make it any easier for you.

It has been said that one of the causes of procrastination is anxiety about the job to be done. However, a great way to overcome this anxiety is actually to face the project head-on and make a start. And don't lose sight of how good you'll feel after completing the work; this feeling may be motivation enough to get you started. The owner of a telephone-answering service in Louisville, Kentucky, hated to make the cold calls he knew were necessary for finding new customers, and continually put off picking up the telephone. He was able to overcome his procrastination by taking a sales training program to learn cold calling techniques and other sales tools.

Stick to Your Schedule

Having a schedule is a great way to become disciplined and avoid procrastination. There's great satisfaction in completing a job so you can check it off your to-do list. Again, scheduling parts of a job at different times rather than the whole job at once can help you get your arms around what might seem to be an insurmountable task.

Follow Through

Become a finisher and complete the tasks before you. A schedule may be useful to starting a task, but it's up to you to complete it.

Use Time-Saving Devices

The Luddites, English factory workers whose jobs were being supplanted by technology in the early 1800s, thought that machines would be the downfall of society. Rioting at factories and even killing a factory owner did not stem the use of machines; the Luddite movement died out in six years, proving machines were here to stay. However, today we recognize that machines don't supplant people; they are here to serve them by freeing them from repetitive activities and giving them more time for other more productive tasks.

Use What You Have Fully

You may already own equipment or tools designed to save you time, but you aren't taking full advantage of their capacity. What office telephone today does not have a speed dial option? Yet many small-business owners never take the time to program in their frequently used telephone numbers. Recognize that the few minutes to program your speed dial can save you hours of time when connecting you to those you call frequently.

Upgrade Equipment

Look around. Are you working with machines that are outdated? They may be slowing you down. Now may be a great time to get rid of the old and bring in the new. For example, if you are working with older computers, you may be wasting precious seconds each time you use a different function, waiting to open or save documents, perform calculations, or create artwork. Or you may have an old CD drive that takes considerable time to burn a CD; you would save minutes, not just seconds, by replacing it with a new rewritable-CD drive. It may well be worth the financial investment to upgrade your equipment in order to save you time.

If you use the Internet frequently, make sure your access is the quickest you can afford. Broadband and T2 enable you to speedily download and upload files, do Web-based research, and conduct lightning-fast e-commerce.

If you use Microsoft products on your business computer, be sure to obtain the latest updates, called patches. A notice usually pops up to alert you to new updates, or go to Microsoft Office Online at http://office.microsoft.com and click on "Office Update;

Check for Updates." This will make your programs run faster and more efficiently.

Get Spam Blockers

A survey by United Kingdom–based Novell found that workers waste 10 to 15 minutes each day dealing with spam e-mail (unsolicited bulk e-mail advertising, some of which may even be pornographic or in a foreign language). What's more, spam is annoying and can even be dangerous when used to steal your identity by eliciting your Social Security number, bank account, or other personal information. Your Internet provider may filter out some spam (although you may have to activate the filter).

Also use software designed to minimize the spam that can get through to you (there are shareware and low-cost products created especially for this purpose that you can easily find through your favorite search engine). Usually these programs don't block the e-mail you'd want to receive. Don't waste any time opening and reading spam e-mail; assume that any unrecognized e-mail sender or subject line is spam and just delete it. There are a number of spam protection software products available, some free (through shareware). For example, Symantec offers free antispam software as part of its small-business bundle of software that includes a firewall (www.symantec.com).

Organize Your Contact Lists

When you meet someone at a networking event or a family gathering who you think might be a prospective customer or a great resource, what do you do with the contact information? A slip of paper with a phone number can easily be lost. Or you might forget the connection when you look at the person's business card months after the meeting. When you want to contact the person in the future, you may waste time hunting down the information or trying to remember why you kept the person's phone number in the first place. Even time for contacting existing customers, longtime vendors, or other business associates can be shortened from the old Rolodex search. A time-saving approach to managing your contacts is to organize them into some type of database.

The database can also be used to streamline your marketing activities (discussed in Chapter 9).

In organizing your contacts, be sure to include some key information (in addition to the usual address, telephone, and e-mail):

- *Category of the contact.* Set up categories for existing customers, prospects, vendors, professional contacts, and personal/family contacts. You might also want other categories for repair people or government contacts (e.g., contractors need to reach building inspectors). Usually, the software you use to set up your database contains an organizational chart to help you access the group or individual you are seeking.

- *Additional information.* Most of the software can accommodate your special needs. For example, you might want to note who referred someone to you, the dates of meetings, or other specific information that can help you with future contacts.

There are numerous options for computerizing your contacts. You can create your own database using spreadsheet software, such as Microsoft Excel. Or your can use software specifically designed for this purpose. Your software options include:

- *Act! 2005.* One of the premier contact organizers, this product allows you to fully customize your contact list. For example, you can display contact history, organize contacts into groups and subgroups, and use up to 60 fields for contact information. The product is synchronized for Palm OS and Pocket PC, so if you enter a contact's information when you're out and about, you can automate entry to your personal computer; information can also be imported from Microsoft Outlook (described earlier in this chapter) and other software products. Cost: $209.99 for a single user; $399 for work groups; additional cost for add-on products. You can automate your data entry with a business card scanner that works in tandem with Act! 2005.

- Also check shareware for free or low-cost software alternatives.

Clean Out Clutter

How much time does it take you to put your hands on an old letter from a customer, an article you cut out of a magazine for later use, a business card of someone you met at a networking event, or an e-mail you received from a vendor? If it takes more than a few seconds of your time, you're wasting precious moments. One reason why it might be taking you longer than a few seconds to locate the material you're looking for is clutter. This can be in your file cabinet, on your Rolodex, in your computer, or on your desk. The best way to save time in the future is to invest some now in clearing out clutter.

There are two types of clutter: the physical clutter created by too many papers or a poor organization system and the mental clutter created by having too many unstructured ideas in your mind. Here are some ways to address both types of clutter so you can maximize your time.

Clean Out File Cabinets and Desktops

Time management experts suggest you "handle paper once." This means deciding what to do with a letter, a note, or other piece of paper when you first see it so that it doesn't contribute to future clutter. While clutter may be inevitable for most people, it can be minimized.

Clutter costs you time. The longer you must look through piles to find the slip of paper you want, the less you can get done in a day. Invest the time now to toss out files you no longer need and papers that are not worth saving.

If your piles of paper are overwhelming, bring in a professional organizer to assist you. The *Wall Street Journal* noted that the typical business executive wastes one hour each day searching for missing information on a messy desk and in files. The money you pay for efficient cleanup can save you money in the long run; you'll spend less of your valuable time on this task and you won't have your emotional baggage involved in the process. You may pay a professional organizer by the hour (usually $50 to $200 per hour) or arrange a flat fee for the job.

RESOURCES

To find a professional organizer, contact:

• National Association of Professional Organizers (www.napo .net and, in the "I am interested in . . . " drop-down menu, click on "Finding an Organizer" to use an automated referral program).

• Professional Organizers Web Ring (POWR) (www.organizers webring.com and click on "Search the POWR Member Directory").

Weed Out Bad Prospects from Your Contact Lists

Small-business owners may meet hundreds of people through networking or make thousands of cold calls. Each of these contacts leaves a trail—on paper or your computer. Even if you organize your contacts into a database, you may waste time accessing those you want to reach or target. Take time to clear out those contacts that will never result in sales. Doing so can save you time in contacting better prospects (you won't have to wade through the dead zone).

Throw Away Unused Reading Material

When it comes to ideas, the information age has produced an embarrassment of riches. But to read each one of the newspapers, magazines, newsletters, and books you collect can be an impossible task. Instead, go through your reading material and save only the information dealing with ideas you intend to act upon. Take a deep breath and toss the rest.

Cut out important items you want to go back to. Consider scanning these items into your computer, thus eliminating clutter. Be sure to organize the items so you can access them easily and quickly.

Reduce Your Ideas to Actions

You may have dozens of great ideas floating around in your head. Review them now so you can stop ruminating on those that will go nowhere. Write down the ideas you want to pursue. Or use software designed to help you organize your ideas, such as Brain-Storm (www.brainstormsw.com). Decide what you're going to do with your ideas by creating a plan of action.

Minimize Interruptions

It's been said that if you work in an office, you are probably interrupted an average of once every eight minutes. And it can take four to five minutes to refocus after each interruption. In the course of a day, this can add up to a significant chunk of time that's wasted.

Interruptions are distractions that eat into your time and ability to handle priority jobs. Get an idea of how often you are interrupted and how much time this costs you daily by jotting down interruptions throughout one day. Total up the interruptions and see how much time you'll gain if you can eliminate them from your day. Then take control of your time by effectively handling interruptions. There are four ways to do this:

1. Erect barriers.

2. Schedule time alone.

3. Create alternatives for handling problems.

4. Terminate interruptions.

Erect Barriers

Prevent someone from intruding on your time by setting up physical partitions that isolate you when you want to be alone. Examples:

- *Close your door.* It may not stop the knocking for important matters, but it will discourage interruptions for socializing.

- *Put up a Do Not Disturb sign.* Again, some interruptions will still occur, but more frivolous ones will be prevented.

- *Hold calls.* Don't take phone calls; let someone else or an answering machine field the calls while you spend uninterrupted time focused on what you want to accomplish.

- *Avoid instant messaging.* While instant messaging is the rage in some companies as an instant means of communication, it is often used to pass on trivial information or gossip and can be a great time waster.

Schedule Time Alone

Let co-workers know that you are not to be disturbed at certain times of the day (e.g., before 9 A.M.) when you are attending to matters from which you do not want to be distracted. These interruption-free periods can be as frequent as you need to accomplish the work you have to do. For example, the owner of a financial planning firm in Stamford, Connecticut, comes to the office at 7:30 each morning to devote half an hour to reading his e-mail, the daily papers, and online news to get his bearings before starting the day. He accepts no interruptions, including phone calls, during his "alone time."

Create Alternatives for Handling Problems

You don't have to deal with every problem in your business if you have others working for you.

- Educate your staff to handle problems so you won't be interrupted about every detail.

- Set up chains of command to deal with issues that need immediate attention. Your second in command, for example, may be equally able to field a customer complaint.

Terminate Interruptions

Despite your best efforts, interruptions will undoubtedly occur. Politely but promptly terminate interruptions. For example, tell the person interrupting you that you have to complete a job by a set deadline, but will get back to him or her as soon as possible.

You may have unscheduled visitors who disrupt your day. You can opt *not* to see them, telling them it's not a convenient time for you. If you choose to see them, set limits on the time you'll have together and then schedule a future appointment for further discussions.

Learn to Say No

One of the toughest things for a small-business owner to do is say no. You're a can-do, take-charge person by nature—that's why you run your own business. But you may be wasting time and creating unnecessary stress by agreeing to do more than you should. This can result in responsibility overload. According to Melissa C. Stopper, MD, "'Stressed-out' people are not poor stress managers." They just have too many commitments. Recognizing the problem is the first step in easing the stress.

Examine Your Responsibilities

As a small-business owner, you may have more responsibilities than you can handle without undue stress. After all, at work the buck stops with you. But some of the responsibilities you accept may be over and above what's necessary.

Examine your daily responsibilities at work. Ask yourself what responsibilities you can assign to someone else (whether or not that person currently exists). If, for example, you currently handle your company's collections, which is clearly a highly stressful activity, consider hiring someone to do this task for you or use an outside collection agency.

Assess your personal responsibilities away from work. Besides family commitments, small-business owners are often active in community affairs, participating in various charitable activities. Some of this work may be motivated by a desire to help; some may be because of business connections or for other reasons. If you have too many outside commitments, recognize that you can't maintain your current level of involvement with all of these organizations and causes. Ask yourself where you can limit the time you spend in this area. Don't feel you're letting anyone down by turning down a new request for participation.

Just Say No

One of the most difficult things that a small-business owner must learn is how to say no. Let others at your company handle their jobs themselves—don't try to do their jobs for them.

When faced with potential responsibilities, such as working for a new charity or heading up a business committee on a trade association, just say no. This can be easier to do if you recognize that you won't be perceived as disinterested or lazy.

Schedule Responsibility-Free Time

The adage "All work and no play makes Jack a dull boy" is something to pay attention to. Take care of yourself so you can better take care of your business. Work into your business schedule some time each day for activities that can reduce your stress and keep you on your game, such as:

- Exercise
- Fun
- Meditation
- Prayer
- Sleep

Plan a Vacation

Be sure to schedule vacation time to rejuvenate your mind and body. According to a 2004 survey from OPEN: The Small Business Network, 66 percent of small-business owners planned a summer vacation, which means that about one-third did not take time off. But experts suggest that vacation time is a necessary part of the business process. It gives you time to:

- *Unwind from day-to-day pressures.* Schedule enough vacation time to factor in the days necessary to wind down from work stress. Most small-business owners say that it takes about three days to decompress.

- *Recharge your creative batteries.* By getting away, you can gain a fresh perspective on your business.

- *Spend time with family.* Small-business owners typically work crazy hours, often shortchanging their families by being away so much. A vacation is an opportunity to reconnect with a spouse and children.

- *Improve your health.* According to the Framingham Heart Study, women who vacationed twice a year lowered their risk of coronary heart disease by 50 percent (30 percent in the case of men) (www.nhlbi.nih.gov/about/framingham/index .html).

Small-business owners often have concerns that their absence will hurt their business. They may miss an opportunity, a customer may not receive the best service, equipment may break down, or other catastrophes might occur. All of these fears are understandable, but none of them are justification for skipping a vacation. Instead, take steps to ensure that things will run as smoothly as possible:

- *Limit your time away.* Most small-business owners don't take more than a week at a time.

- *Inform important clients and customers that you will be away.* Give them the name of a person you'd like them to contact if necessary in your absence.

- *Keep in touch through e-mail and by telephone.* According to the OPEN survey, 37 percent of vacationing small-business owners planned to contact the business at least once a day (only 20 percent planned *not* to stay in touch).

Purchase trip-cancellation insurance so that if problems arise that force you to end your vacation early, you won't lose all your travel money.

LESSONS ON MANAGING YOUR TIME

✔ Understand the importance of time management.

✔ Schedule your time to maximize the use of your day.

✔ Learn to share your workload by delegating.

✔ Don't let procrastination undermine your efforts.

✔ Take advantage of technology to save time.

✔ Reduce clutter.

✔ Cut down on interruptions.

✔ Learn to say no.

✔ Schedule free time.

PART TWO

THE FINANCIAL SIDE
OF BUSINESS

Monitor Cash Flow

Money, which represents the prose of life, and which is hardly spoken of in parlors without an apology, is, in its effects and laws, as beautiful as roses.

—Ralph Waldo Emerson

ash flow is nothing more than the movement of money in and out of your business. But in reality it is the lifeblood of your company. You need money to pay your vendors, landlord, and employees in order to stay in business.

As the term implies, cash flow is a moving target; money is constantly going in and out of the business so it can be difficult to pinpoint what your cash status is at any given time. The point of tracking cash flow isn't to get a fix on your money. Rather, it is simply to make sure that there's enough money on tap when you need it.

Cash flow is not the same as profit. Your business may be profitable, yet face a serious cash flow problem. So it isn't helpful to focus only on your bottom line and ignore your money supply.

In this chapter you will gain a better understanding of what cash flow is all about and how you can analyze your company's cash flow cycle so you can predict your future money needs. You'll find out how to plan so that you don't run out of money, and you'll learn about a number of ways in which you can improve your cash flow by increasing the money that comes into your business and decreasing the money that goes out.

Understand the Cash Flow Cycle

How does your cash flow run? As strong and as constant as the Mississippi River or as small and erratic as the little stream that sometimes dries up in the summertime? It is important to know about your company's cash flow so that you can pay your bills to stay in business.

Cash Flow

Cash flow is the cycle of money going in and out of your company. Usually, it is tracked from the start of the sales process. As a general rule, money flows out during the first phase of the cycle when you incur expenses to furnish your goods or services and flows in during the final phase when you collect the payment for sales. The first phase of the cycle erodes your cash stash; the final phase replenishes it. In other words, the cycle is the time it takes to convert a sale into cash.

Let's take an example. A small specialty-clothing manufacturer buys fabric to make the clothes (paying vendors in about 30 days). The clothes are manufactured to become part of inventory; then the inventory must be sold and shipped to retailers. During this time, there are ongoing labor costs and other overhead expenses (including principal and interest payments on outstanding loans), as well as shipping costs. The retailers are billed immediately, but it may be 30 days, 90 days, or more from the billing date before payment is received. The cash flow cycle of this company can easily be six months or even longer.

A CPA who does tax returns may have a very short cash flow cycle. She may perform the work, bill for the services, and receive payment all within the course of a few weeks or a month. In contrast, a personal injury attorney may incur expenses for a case that may take years to resolve (and perhaps longer to collect fees). Each business is different. Each business has a different cash flow profile because each business has unique abilities of selling, billing, and collecting money.

Cash Flow Analysis

Do you know how long it takes for money to come in during your business cycle? Without this knowledge you may be caught short of the cash needed to meet your obligations. Take the case of a wedding planner in Seattle. She was great at creating a bride's dream event, but couldn't get her mind around cash flow. As a planner she could schedule every component of the event, from the caterer and photographer, to the invitation printer and band. But she failed to take a sufficient down payment from the bride's father to cover the deposits she owed to each player involved in the affair, leaving her dreadfully short of money to pay her own bills.

Cash flow analysis, which is also called cash flow projection or forecasting, involves an examination of the income coming in and the expenses for which money goes out. It lets you know how much money you'll need at some future point to meet your expenses.

Cash flow analysis also involves the time span in which these items occur. In an ideal situation, you hope your cash outflow will be less than your cash inflow, or will match as closely as possible. If outflow is more than inflow, the wider the gap between these events, the more problematic things can become.

Experts differ on how long you need cash flow projections for. Some suggest that six months out is long enough, while others say that two years are mandatory. Obviously, you must find what will work best for you.

Keep a Close Eye on Cash Flow

As the owner of your business, it's your responsibility to keep tabs on cash flow. Whether you work with an accountant or have a board of directors or advisers, it is ultimately up to you to watch your money and initiate appropriate steps if there are cash flow problems.

In the old (precomputer) days, monitoring cash flow required a time-consuming projection on paper of your money needs, month by month. Doing this work the old-fashioned way—as an exercise—may help you better understand what cash flow is all about. The worksheet in Table 5.1 shows how to perform this analysis for the month of January; you would do the same analysis for each of the other 11 months of the year.

TABLE 5.1 Monthly Cash Flow Analysis Worksheet

	January

Cash in (what you have on hand at the start of the month):
    Cash in the bank
    Petty cash	

+ Cash sales throughout the month	
+ Accounts receivable paid in the month for sales made this month and in prior months	
= Total cash in	
− Disbursements (payments for monthly rent and other overhead expenses as well as other payments for the month)	
= Cash balance (the difference between your money in and money out for the month)	

Today, monitoring cash flow can be automated with the use of software designed for this purpose. This cuts down considerably on the time it takes to track your money. If you work closely with an accountant, it is the job of this professional to closely watch your cash flow and to advise you if there is a problem.

If you keep your own books, then use software to help you track your cash flow. For example, if you use QuickBooks to keep your books, you can find there two useful cash flow reports: Statement of Cash Flows and Cash Flow Forecast. You do nothing to complete these reports; they are filled in automatically based on the income and expenses you input to your books. All you have to do is be sure that you check these reports regularly to detect problems on the horizon. Other small-business accounting software, such as M.Y.O.B. Accounting and Peachtree First Accounting, have similar cash flow reports and tracking.

You can also use software whose main function is to track and analyze cash flow.

RESOURCES

Examples of cash flow analysis software:

- Cash Compass from Palo Alto Software (www.bplans .com) helps you monitor your cash flow, manage your budgets, and make forecasts on a monthly or yearly basis. Cost: $199.

- Freeware and shareware software on cash flow planning is also available from Business PlanWare at www.planware .org.

- Specialized software by industry (e.g., Landlord's Cash Flow Analyzer Pro at www.landlordsoftware.com and Up Your Cash Flow—Contractor at www.cashplan.com).

Plan for Adequate Cash Flow

Lack of capital is one of the main reasons that businesses fail. They run out of the money needed to pay their bills, and creditors can force them into bankruptcy, requiring them to liquidate the business and distribute whatever money there is to those creditors. It doesn't matter that there is a hot sales prospect in the wings or that the long-range forecast for the business is great. You need to have adequate sources of money to pay your bills when they come due.

Thus, it is essential that you keep a close eye on your cash flow. Detecting problems early gives you time to make the necessary changes (discussed later in this chapter) so that disaster can be averted. At the very least, you should be able to know at all times how much cash you have on hand and what the business needs to operate. The term *cash* doesn't mean only a stack of currency in your petty-cash box. It includes all of the ways you can access money, including funds in your business checking account and the company line of credit that you can draw upon to pay the bills.

Warning Signs of a Cash Flow Problem

You may not perform an in-depth cash flow analysis each and every month, but you can stay on top of things and avoid a potential problem by doing an easy check at the end of each month. Compare your sales with your expenses. If your expenses, including overhead and purchases to make your sales, are outpacing your sales, you have a potential problem.

Danger signs that you may have or are about to have a cash problem include:

- *Bank account balances drop below normal averages.* Check the balances on your business checking and savings accounts each month to see that they approximate what you have been seeing in prior months. A decline does not necessarily mean you're in trouble; you may simply have purchased new equipment or made an unusual purchase. But if there is a decline for an unexplained reason, it may indicate cash flow problems (e.g., that your expenses have gone up without the same increase in sales).

- *Sales outlook is dim.* Depending on your type of business, you may continually have sales in the pipeline. For example, if you are an architect, you prepare proposals in order to keep new sales forthcoming. But if you notice that you are doing fewer proposals, you will probably have less sales in the future, something that can jeopardize your cash flow stability.

- *Inventory is building up.* If you find items are sitting on your shelf for longer and longer periods, again you face an issue of reduced sales, which will bring in less revenue.

- *Bills are being paid late.* Many bills you receive are due on receipt or within 10 days. Some bills may give you a 30-day period in which to remit payment. If you find that you are paying these bills in 60 days, 90 days, or longer, you know there's already a serious cash flow problem.

- *Major purchases are being postponed.* Your company needs a piece of equipment, but you can't afford to buy it now because money is tight.

- *Banks are asking for financial statements.* You already have outstanding commercial loans and your lenders are getting nervous, as evidenced by their requests for your balance sheets, income statements, and other financial information.

Z-Score

If you want to get technical and work the math, you can use a formula developed in 1968 by Edward Altman as a predictor of the likelihood of bankruptcy, a common result from poor cash flow. (If math isn't your forte or you don't want to run the numbers, you can show your accountant this formula.) The Z-Score formula (as modified in 1977) is:

$$Z = 1.2(A) + 1.4(B) + 3.3(C) + 0.6(D)$$

where A = Working capital/Total assets (working capital is the capital available to the business on the short term, figured by subtracting current liabilities from current assets)

  B = Retained earnings/Total assets (retained earnings are the accumulated profits of the business that are not distributed to owners)

  C = Earnings before interest and taxes/Total assets

  D = Book value/Total liabilities (book value is the value of a company's assets as carried on its balance sheet)

If the Z-Score is above 2.99, bankruptcy is unlikely. But if it is between 1.81 and 2.99 there is a possibility of bankruptcy; a score of 1.8 or less indicates a high probability of bankruptcy.

Example: A manufacturing company has working capital of $100, total assets of $1,000, retained earnings of $400, earnings before interest and taxes of $50, book value of $600, and total liabilities of $700. Crunching the numbers in this case results in a Z-Score of 1.359 [1.2($100/$1,000) + 1.4 ($400/$1,000) + 3.3 ($50/$1,000) + 0.6($600/$700], which indicates very serious trouble.

If working capital had been $500 rather than $100, the Z-Score would be 1.839, well within the iffy category; working capital of

$1,500 would put the Z-Score at 3.039, comfortably within the un-likelihood-of-bankruptcy category.

Improve Cash Flow

Just because you see a cash flow problem looming does not mean you are doomed to experience difficulties. Knowing that there's a potential problem lets you take steps to avoid a crisis. There are two main ways to improve your cash flow: Increase the amount of cash that's coming in and reduce the amount of cash that's flowing out. Both ways help to ensure that you won't run out of cash. It is usually advisable to tackle both ways simultaneously in order to avoid a cash crunch.

Cash Reserves

If possible (and for many small businesses this is virtually im-possible to do), create a cash reserve to help you ride out the lows you may experience. A cash reserve will help you avoid the need to take drastic measures when you experience a cash flow problem.

Warning: Pay Taxes First

In managing cash flow, *always* avoid problems with the IRS and state sales tax departments. Pay your tax obligations before other creditors, even if the other creditors are knocking at the door. If certain taxes are in arrears (check with your accountant as to which taxes you must pay immediately), these government agencies can freeze your bank account and/or seize your assets. By then it may be too late to address your cash flow difficulties. Once your accounts are frozen, you are no longer in a control of your money.

Strategies for Increasing Cash Inflow

Short of winning the lottery, receiving an inheritance, or depleting your nest egg and putting the funds into your business, there's no fast and easy way to boost your company's money supply. Generally, you must look to increase your sales and the collection of payments on these sales. There are, however, other ways to increase your money supply besides boosting sales or putting more of your own money into the business. You can also increase the return on your investments (e.g., interest on money market accounts) and look to find financing from loans, factoring (similar to loans), or grants.

Increase Sales

Obviously, if you sell more, you'll take in more cash through these sales. Thus, the first and main way to increase your money supply is to take steps to boost your sales, such as changing and rearranging marketing efforts.

However, recognizing the old adage "It takes money to make money," stepping up your sales efforts may initially cost you more than you take in. You'll have to pay at the start of the sales cycle for these additional costs even though you may not see a return until later on. Thus, it's a good idea to launch this approach well before you face serious cash flow problems.

Raise Prices

Review your current pricing schedule to see if there is room to make upward adjustments. When was the last time you raised prices? If it was more than a year ago, it may well be time to revise your pricing schedule. What are your competitors charging? You may have fallen behind in pricing by not raising your fees sooner. How is the economy doing? A booming economy can better support your price increases than one in a recession.

In deciding how much to raise the prices on the goods and services you sell, factor in price increases that you've experienced. Your insurance costs may have risen, your rent increased, you raised employee wages, all of which are a bigger drag on your cash flow. The rise in gasoline prices in 2005 has severely harmed some small businesses, especially those that find it difficult to pass on price increases to customers. A restaurant owner in Richmond, Virginia, had to pay a surcharge for every food delivery—$2 here, $3 there—until the weekly delivery costs became a problem. He couldn't just raise menu prices across the board and risk losing customers. He found a creative way to pass on the added fuel surcharge by raising prices only on special catered events. If costs escalate, you must raise prices somehow just to stay even, much less to continue making a profit.

Also examine your profit margin—how much you make on each unit you sell. If you routinely maintain a 20 percent profit margin, check your prices to see that they continue to support this rate. Increased costs may have diminished your profit margin and you may be justified in raising prices now.

How much and how often you can raise prices depends on your competitors, the economy, and, of course, your customers. A service business may routinely raise prices annually; a retail store may boost prices on some items every few months but keep prices steady on others.

There are different strategies for raising prices. One school of thought supports a big jump on the theory that customers will get over the pain, as long as you don't inflict it too often. However, others introduce price hikes in gradual steps to lessen the impact on customers. There is also the thought that smaller hikes may go unnoticed. And there is also a valid argument for *cutting* prices in order to drive up volume sales. This alternative strategy may work for some businesses, depending on the type of things they sell.

After deciding how much (and how often), then decide *when* to introduce the new pricing. It is common for many retailers to increase prices in the fall before the Christmas shopping season gets under way. High-tech businesses may raise prices with the introduction of new models, rather than at any particular time of the year. Determine what is the right course of action for your industry.

When raising prices, consider how to add value to your product or service in order to lessen the impact of the price increase. For example, you may be able to add a freebie to accompany the sale of a product that has just had a price boost.

In tandem with raising prices, you should examine your discounting policy (if you have one). It may be time to eliminate or reduce your discounts.

Improve Collection of Receivables

You may want to review your collection policies and become more aggressive about delinquent accounts. There are also incentives you can use to obtain payments more rapidly and to avoid slow-paying and nonpaying customers. The topic of collections is discussed in Chapter 6.

Tighten or Loosen Up on Extending Credit to Customers

Always try to get cash up front to avoid extending credit to customers. But this is not always possible. For example, if you are a Web designer who contracts to create a Web presence for a company, you may receive payment upon completion of the job. However, you can usually arrange to receive partial payment at stages of the job, including 25 percent to 50 percent of the total fee up front.

In some industries, however, it may be common for sellers to let buyers purchase on credit. Without this policy, you may well lose some business. But you should assess the true cost of this policy. Presumably, you are compensated for the credit arrangement by having the buyer repay not only the cost of the sale, but also the cost of the credit (interest). But this may not fully compensate you. There is an added cost to extending credit: the cost of collection—your efforts to make sure you receive what you're owed and the problems that arise when you cannot collect all that you are owed.

If you decide to extend credit, review the type of credit checks you do on potential customers who want to buy on credit. Raise the bar on who you will give credit to or lower the bar if your credit policy is too stringent. Also consider placing a dollar limitation on the amount of credit you are willing to extend.

Maximize Investment Returns

If you are fortunate enough to be sitting on cash reserves, don't let them sit idle. Invest (carefully). Make your money work for you, but choose investments that keep your money liquid so you can use the funds as needed at any time. For example, depending on the size of your reserve, you may invest in money market mutual funds or short-term commercial paper.

Find Grant Money

While there may not be an abundance of grants for small businesses, this financing mechanism should certainly be explored. Grants are free money because they do not have to be repaid.

To find grants for small business, go to the Small Business Administration's portal to federal grants at www.sba.gov/expanding/ grants.html. Also inquire at your state and local level about grant opportunities.

Borrow Money

You don't have to take out a loan and keep the money sitting in the bank to be in a good position to avoid a cash flow disaster. All you need is to put financing options in place so that you can call upon them when necessary. It is always better to make these arrangements when you are in a good financial position than to wait until you really need the money. Consider the following financing options.

LINE OF CREDIT

Set up a pot of money you can draw upon as needed. A line of credit is a loan you obtain from your bank up to a fixed limit. Usually, this type of loan is a revolving line. As you pay back principal you have more to draw on later on. The line runs for a set term, but can be extended as needed if the bank is agreeable.

FACTORING

If your business has accounts receivable that you must wait to collect upon, consider using a company, called a factor, that will buy your receivables (outstanding invoices) from you. Factoring originally was used exclusively in the clothing industry, but today it is being used by many different businesses. The amount you receive has nothing to do with your creditworthiness, but rather the creditworthiness of businesses that owe you money. With factoring, you'll receive 50 percent to 80 percent of the receivables' face value up front. The factor then collects on the receivables and remits to you the amount collected, less the factor's fee. This fee is usually 1 percent to 5 percent of the face value of the receivables. So, in effect, you may receive up to 99 percent of what you are owed, with the bonus of getting half or more of those funds immediately for working capital. Using a factor can be a short-term arrangement to help you over a rough spot. But some small businesses, especially those with continual cash flow swings resulting from seasonal payroll or peak sales periods, may work with a factor as a long-term arrangement. Try to obtain "nonrecourse" on the financing so that the up-front money is yours, even if the factor fails to collect on one or more of the receivables. It is usually a good idea to work with a broker specializing in factoring (and who is compensated by a finder's fee that may be pricey). The broker can shop around for the best factoring company for you and help negotiate the best deal. To locate a broker, do an Internet search in your favorite search engine for "factoring brokers" (make sure you are dealing with a broker and not a factoring company). To check on a factor, contact the Commercial Finance Association (CFA), a trade association for the asset-based financial services industry (www.cfa.com and click on "Member Roster" to search by state).

FINANCING FROM SUPPLIERS

Your vendors may be able to offer you extended payment terms, minimizing your current need for cash. For example, ask for 180-day payment terms. Of course, this will cost you more overall if there are financing costs, but it can help you get over the hump.

Strategies for Decreasing Cash Outflow

You can improve your cash flow by minimizing the drain on your money supply. Usually this means tightening your belt. But there are also a number of creative ways to reduce or delay the outflow of cash from your business.

Cut Expenses

Obviously, the less money you spend, the less you need to take in and the better your cash flow will be. But reducing expenses can be challenging, especially if it requires laying off a valued employee or waiting another year to buy a needed piece of equipment.

Examine carefully *everything* you spend money on; there's surely room for savings. Try to renegotiate the cost of products or services you regularly purchase since these sellers may be willing to work with you to keep you as a satisfied customer.

Buy smarter. The less you pay for something, the better off you will be. Today, you can check the prices of everything from supplies to heavy machinery at online sites such as eBay (www.ebay.com) and may, in fact, save money by making your purchases online through auction sites or remainder sellers.

If you are experiencing severe cash flow problems, you may have to make drastic and painful cuts. You may, for example, need to scale back wages (at least temporarily) in order to avoid firings.

Caution: Do not overlook your obligation to pay so-called trust fund taxes—this is not the place to cut. Trust fund taxes are payroll taxes you withhold on behalf of your employees (income taxes and the employee share of Social Security and Medicare taxes). No matter how your business is legally organized, you are personally liable for 100 percent of these funds. You do not want to pay another creditor over the U.S. Treasury in this case.

Trim Inventory

If you sell goods, you have an inventory on hand for sale. Ideally, you can switch to a just-in-time inventory management system where you do not stock anything until it is needed. You might, for example, be able to arrange shipment directly from a manufacturer rather than warehousing items yourself. But most businesses can't do this, so you might want to aim for minimizing the amount of inventory you carry. Again, this is simply a matter of cutting back—ordering less and stocking a smaller variety of items. Of course, you must maintain sufficient inventory to offer your customers a good selection of items and be able to deliver promptly, so scaling back requires some finesse. Also work with suppliers to increase delivery time for your receipt of inventory items so you can cut back on your stockpiles.

Use Barter

Instead of paying for goods or services you need, arrange to obtain them in trade for the things you sell. Contrary to what you may think, barter did not disappear with the old trading post. It is used regularly by over 65 percent of Fortune 500 companies and about 470,000 companies, large and small, worldwide that do more than $1 billion in trade, according to the International Reciprocal Trade Association (IRTA).

You can barter directly with another party, making a one-on-one exchange. For example, if you own a restaurant, you may barter for advertising space in your local newspaper. You exchange coupons for meals or discounts and receive advertising for your restaurant in the newspaper.

Alternatively you can work through a barter exchange. This is a local or national organization with members or clients that contact each other or the exchange itself to jointly trade or barter goods or services. Using a barter exchange gives you more flexibility to obtain the things you want for the things you have to trade through a process called "round robin." For instance, say you are a chiropractor who needs a computer for the office. You can build up credits at the exchange by offering your services to other members in the exchange; you can cash in your credits for a computer sold by someone in the exchange who traded the machine to obtain cleaning services for his store. You can find a barter exchange by doing an Internet search for "barter exchanges." Check the cost of membership and transaction fees before joining an exchange. Membership fees and transaction costs can easily add 10 percent to the price of what you acquire. At America Barters (www.americabarters .com), you pay a flat monthly fee of $40, regardless of the number of transactions you do.

Another way of bartering is to set up local trading circles in your area. For example, if you have a store in a mall, merchants can agree to barter among other merchants there. There are no fees as in the case of a barter exchange, but your network is limited.

Bartering may become so attractive that you are tempted to try to work exclusively in this manner. It is common, however, to limit bartering to 5 percent to 15 percent of your business, and most experts advise against exceeding 25 percent.

Caution: Bartering doesn't save you any taxes. The products or services you trade away are considered taxable sales just as if you'd received cash (rather than bartered goods or services). This means you include the sales in your income. You may also pay sales taxes on the items you acquire. Typically, you pay the seller separately for the sales tax on the item you acquire by barter. On the flip side, the items you acquire via trade may be tax-deductible business expenses as they would be if you had paid cash for them.

Also, the law limits what you can and cannot barter, so check with an attorney if you have any questions. For example, the law bans bartering of banking services, insurance, and publicly traded stock.

Delay Paying Your Bills

You don't want to fall delinquent on your obligations—doing so can cost you interest charges, damage your credit rating, and cause you to lose standing with existing vendors or suppliers. But you don't have to pay immediately. Take advantage of the payment terms. For example, if you have a 30-day window, remit payment on the 27th day. Pick and choose carefully which creditors to pay if funds are tight, paying careful attention to interest rates that may apply.

Use online payment options to finely time your payments. Since transfers are instantaneous, you can send payments at the very last minute.

If you must be late, talk with your suppliers to gain their understanding. Try to arrange for extended payment options, even if it costs you some interest charges, if you are experiencing a temporary cash crunch.

LESSONS ABOUT CASH FLOW

✔ The cash flow cycle is the lifeblood of your business.

✔ It is your responsibility, as the business owner, to monitor cash flow and initiate strategies to avoid problems.

✔ Do (or have your accountant do) cash flow projections for at least six months out and keep a close eye on them.

✔ Watch for warning signs that you are facing cash flow problems.

✔ Take action to increase the cash that flows into your business.

✔ Take action to decrease the cash that flows out from your business.

Extend Credit and Stay on Top of Collections

The creditor has a better memory than the debtor.
—James Howell (British historical writer
who died in 1666)

ometimes earning money is easier than collecting it. Customers can eagerly gobble up what you provide to them, but may be slow or downright resistant to paying you. This creates collection problems for you, leading to wasted time and lost revenue that can undermine your company's success.

First determine whether your business is an accounts receivable type of company—a business that sells something and then bills for it, carrying an outstanding accounts receivable on its books until payment is collected. If your business doesn't fit this profile—if instead money changes hands at the time you make a sale—you can ignore this chapter. But if you include an invoice when you make the sale and allow customers time to pay you some or all of what is owed, pay close attention. It is vital to recognize the importance of using smart collection policies to minimize the number of slow payments and nonpayments you experience.

According to nationwide estimates, you can expect that about 18 percent of your customers are typically slow payers, and as many as 2 percent have no intention of ever paying. This means you must go into collections with your eyes open and be prepared to take decisive action in order to get paid.

In this chapter you will learn not only the importance of collections, but also how to find out about your customer before you even make a sale and how to use smart invoicing policies to start you on the road to solid collections. You'll see how to accept alternative forms of payment as a convenience to your customers, which is a way to ensure that you are compensated for the things you sell. And you'll find out what steps can be taken when collections become delinquent.

Importance of Collections

You sell something—a handbag, an architectural design, a repair to a leaky pipe—and you expect to be paid. You've done your part and now it's for the customer to settle up. For some businesses, payments occur simultaneously with the sale; in a seamless transaction in which goods or services are exchanged. But in other businesses, it is customary to provide the goods and services first and wait for payment later.

You know your business and which category of seller you fall into. If it's the latter and you don't usually receive payment immediately, then take appropriate steps to ensure that you'll receive full payment in the time period you expect. It is vital to your company that you receive timely payments; slow payments adversely affect your cash flow (see Chapter 5), which jeopardizes your ability to pay your suppliers and other people to whom you owe money.

Most small businesses experience some problems when it comes to collections. Slow collections not only pose a cash flow problem for you. They also eat up your time and efforts that could better be spent making sales and growing your business. If you or an employee must spend hours each day tracking down tardy customers, company productivity lags.

If you fail to collect payment for merchandise you sell, you can write off your losses for tax purposes as adjustments to inventory amounts or as fully deductible business bad debts. This can make you whole (almost). But if you are a service business on the cash method of accounting (you report income when received and deduct expenses when paid), you lose out completely if you fail to collect on outstanding accounts receivable. You cannot deduct what is owed for your time. For example, a dentist fills a tooth but the customer never pays the bill. This professional worked for nothing: no revenue and not even a tax deduction for his/her trouble.

Know Your Customer

It's a free country, so you can pick and choose with whom you do business (as long as you don't discriminate against a class of customers). Usually, this isn't something you delve into too deeply (or at all); you merely make a sale. But if your type of business allows customers to pay sizable invoices on terms (e.g., 30 days or more) or extends credit to customers, then make sure you know with whom you're dealing.

Just as major banks and finance companies check out prospective borrowers before granting a loan or financing a sale through installment payments, you can do some investigation about prospective customers. Learn whether they have the ability to pay the bill. You can't use a crystal ball to make this determination, but you can rely on a review of their prior credit history to see if the customer has a responsible payment pattern so that you can decide whether you'll work with a customer. Use a credit risk management company such as Dun & Bradstreet (D&B).

RESOURCES

One of the best-known sources for checking business backgrounds is Dun & Bradstreet. Small businesses can use D&B Small Business Solutions to do an online search of its database (http://smallbusiness.dnb.com). You can then choose from a menu of services that include a comprehensive report (at $139.99) and a Credit eValuator Report (at $29.99). If you use D&B reports frequently, you can become a subscriber so that the price of each report is free or discounted (depending on your subscriber level); the subscription categories start at $9.99 per month.

Important: In addition to credit reports, D&B can also monitor your customers' accounts to receive alerts if there are changes that may affect collections. For example, if one of your customers is sued, you can be notified of this event, something that could affect the customer's ability to pay you.

Use Smart Invoicing Policies

Before you perform any services or ship any products, examine your invoicing policies. You may be able to adopt practices that help to ensure you'll receive prompt payment. Here are some important ideas to incorporate in your business practices.

Put Your Terms in Writing

Your written agreement to perform services or sell goods is a legally binding contract spelling out your performance obligations and your customer's payment obligations. In order to create an effective contract, you must spell out your terms carefully. Have your agreement reviewed by an attorney before the customer signs it.

Reward Those Who Prepay

You may want to give up a little to make sure you get a lot. For example, offer a 5 percent discount to customers who pay 100 percent up front, eliminating the need to send an invoice. The $500 you give up on a $10,000 job could easily be justified by the time you won't have to spend invoicing and following up on collections.

Bill in Installments

If you are doing a job over a period of time, be sure to arrange to be paid in stages rather than to receive full payment only upon completion. This ensures that you effectively collect on a pay-as-you-go basis—and limits your possible loss to a portion of your work.

If customers are resistant, offer a money-back guarantee if you fail to meet certain expectations. This leaves you holding the money and negotiating a refund if the customer is dissatisfied.

Prepare a Great Invoice

Make sure your invoice contains *all* of the following features:

- The word "Invoice" in large, bold letters to let your customer know the correspondence is a demand for payment.

- Reference to the purchase order or contract number and a brief description of the goods and/or services provided so that there's no confusion about what the invoice relates to.

- A breakdown of how much is due and when. If you want immediate payment say "Payment due upon receipt of invoice." Otherwise state your terms of payment (e.g., "net seven days" or "net 30 days"). If you offer a discount for immediate payment (see preceding subsections), state this on the invoice, specifying the savings to your customer.

Use Software to Automate Your Invoicing

Save time (and the cost of postage) by generating invoices through your bookkeeping software and sending them via e-mail. This procedure also ensures that your customer will receive it and you won't hear that it got "lost in the mail." You can also combine automated invoicing with the option to pay you online (see payment alternatives section that follows).

Make Paying Simple

The easier you can make the payment process for a customer, the more assured you will be of receiving payment promptly. For example, enclose a self-addressed, stamped envelope and two copies of the invoice (one to be returned to you with payment).

Offer Payment Alternatives

You can sidestep the need to bill for your goods and services by offering customers the option to pay by credit (or debit) card or use collect on delivery (COD). Another alternative is to use a postdated check where the customer writes a check that you can cash or deposit on a date in the future. While a postdated check is not legal until the payment date on the check, it is a common business practice and avoids the need to go back to a customer to ask for payment.

Accept Credit Card Payments

Over 80 percent of American households now use at least one credit card and, according to American Consumer Credit Counseling, tend to spend more than when paying cash. You can accept payment by credit cards, such as American Express, Discover, MasterCard, or Visa. If you do so, provide room on the invoice to include key credit card information (card type, account number, expiration date, and an authorized signature). Encourage customers to return completed invoices to you by fax (rather than mail) so you can immediately process the payment.

In accepting credit (or debit) cards, you have to get merchant authorization status. This allows you to process credit card payments. You can ask your bank or use an independent company to set up a merchant account for this purpose.

Once this is done, you can process payments through a credit card terminal, by telephone, or online (which requires encryption technology to protect the privacy of your customers and you), or you can use a combination. Whichever method you select, there is a cost involved. Check out:

- *Equipment costs*—to buy or rent a point-of-sale terminal (a little box that processes credit card transactions through your telephone line).

- *The discount rate*—the percentage of each sale that you owe to the company through which you pass your credit card transactions (e.g., your bank). For example, you may owe MasterCard 2 percent of the amount charged, so that if your customer charges $1,000, you keep $980 and MasterCard gets $20. The discount rate for most small businesses (with modest transaction levels) can run from 2 percent to 5.5 percent of sales, with higher charges for American Express.

- *Setup fee*—the initial cost to get you started (typically around $200).

- *Transaction fees*—costs to process payments (collect from the credit card company and deposit funds into your bank account). This is a per-transaction charge, with a minimum monthly fee (for small businesses that have fewer than 1,000 transactions a month, the cost may be around $25 each month).

Caution: Just because you accept payment by credit card doesn't mean you can feel totally secure about payment. If the buyer disputes the charges, you can experience a "chargeback," where the credit card company recoups the funds it had previously disbursed to you. And, if you experience a high number of chargebacks, your merchant authorization may be canceled.

Offer PayPal

A credit card alternative that can be especially attractive to small businesses is PayPal, a company that is the largest online payment system and which is now owned by eBay. The company started as a way for eBay buyers to easily pay for things purchased on the site. For sellers it is easy to become authorized to accept PayPal as a payment method, and today about 90 percent of all eBay sellers accept PayPal. At present, only a modest number of small businesses use PayPal outside of eBay, but expect to see the use of this payment method grow.

To add PayPal to your payment method repertoire, you merely have to link an online account at PayPal to your bank (for details on setting up an account, go to www.paypal.com and click on "Business Account").

From a cost perspective, accepting payment through PayPal may be less expensive than credit cards. You do not need any special equipment nor need to pay any setup fees. Your only expense is a per-transaction charge, which is a flat 30-cent fee plus a percentage of the transaction amount (as high as 2.9 percent for amounts up to $3,000 and as low as 1.9 percent for amounts over $100,000). In comparison, credit card percentages do not vary with the size of the transaction, so whatever you agree to pay, that's your cost for the sale.

Unlike credit card processing, the funds from PayPal are deposited into your PayPal account. You can access the funds by transferring them to your bank account (you can do this online for no cost; the transfer takes three to four days). Other ways to access PayPal funds include receiving a check (there's a $1.50 charge per check), shop with a debit card issued by PayPal, get cash at an ATM machine through a PayPal debit card, or purchase supplies and equipment needed for your business from a seller that accepts PayPal (there are more than 42,000 web sites that accept PayPal).

Sell COD

Formerly called cash on delivery but now called collect on delivery, this payment method does not release items to a buyer until payment is made to the shipping company; the payment is then remitted to you. The buyer must pay the shipper upon delivery with a personal check, money order or certified check (some shippers accept only certified checks) to complete the transaction.

RESOURCES

- FedEx Collect on Delivery can be combined with Priority or Standard Overnight or 2Day, Express Saver, or Express Freight (but not with SameDay or First Overnight delivery) (go to www.fedex.com/us/services/options/express/cod.html).

- UPS C.O.D. Enhancement Services include C.O.D. Automatic, which transfers funds to your bank account within two to three days after delivery, and C.O.D. Secure, which guarantees payment to you up to a set limit (go to http://capital.ups.com and click on "Solutions," then "C.O.D. Enhancement Services").

- USPS Collect on Delivery can be used for items up to $1,000 and can be combined with Express Mail (www.usps.com, click on "All Products & Services," then "Collect on Delivery (COD)").

Even though this was called cash on delivery, cash can no longer be used for payment.

The seller pays the COD fee. For United States Postal Service (USPS) delivery, the fee ranges from $4.50 for amounts up to $50 to $14.50 for amounts from $900.01 to $1,000. The post office will not accept COD on amounts over $1,000. Amounts can include both the cost of the merchandise and the postage. For United Parcel Service (UPS), the fees vary with your level of business with the company (you have to ask for a quote).

Get Slow-Paying Customers to Ante Up

The longer you delay following up on late payments, the smaller your chances of receiving a full recovery. Statistics compiled by the Commercial Collection Agency Association (CCAA) show that on the date an account is due, you are likely to collect 98.8 percent of the money you are owed; but any money owed after just three months has only a 73 percent chance of collection; after six months, 57 percent; after one year, 29 percent; and after 24 months, the likelihood of collection drops to about 11.2 percent.

Establish collection policies that you will follow through on. For example, if you give customers a 30-day window in which to pay, then decide that if you have received no payment within 30 days of the date of the invoice, you will set your collection process in motion. The type of policy you adopt depends in part on the nature of your business.

You can simply reinvoice your late-paying customers, marking the invoice as past due. Or you can send a letter referring to the original invoice and noting that the customer is late in making the payment.

Instead of sending letters, which are often ignored, try e-mail. This method can easily resolve such problems as the nonreceipt of the original invoice by the customer. If the amount outstanding justifies your time, a personal phone call may be effective—especially when the customer is ready and able to pay but has lost the invoice (or never received it).

For very small companies where all aspects of business activities are in the hands of one person or only a few people, create a "billing department" to make customers sit up and take notice of your collection efforts. Be sure to give them the name of your "department head" to get back to so that you can track these efforts. The owner and sole employee of a copier and printer repair company in Tampa, Florida, created a separate voice mailbox on his answering machine for his billing department.

Even if you have set up great collection policies and followed them to the letter, there are inevitably some customers who will remain delinquent. You need to be creative in these circumstances to collect what's owed to you.

- Be persistent but don't be belligerent if you want to maintain a business relationship with the customer. If you're doing business with large corporations, you may be at their mercy when it comes to collections (they'll pay you at their convenience because they know you need their continued business).

- Arrange for extended payment terms if customers are experiencing cash flow problems. Be sure to formalize the terms in a signed promissory note or written payment plan. The note or plan should include an interest factor to compensate you for the customer's use of your money. The benefit of using a promissory note is that customers know they won't be hounded for collection if they live up to its terms, but if they don't you can sue.

Working with Collection Agencies

If, despite all your best invoicing policies and collection efforts, you fail to see satisfactory results in four to six months, you may want to turn to an outsider to take over collection efforts for you. Collection agencies specialize in obtaining payments on outstanding accounts receivable.

What to Look For When Engaging a Collection Agency

There are many fish in the sea of collection agencies, so only hook one that meets your requirements. Usually you want to work with a company that has the experience to be successful on your behalf (e.g., has been in business for at least five years). Also make sure the collection agency:

- Is licensed in your state and in every state in which it will be collecting money for you.

- Provides a surety bond (look for a minimum of $300,000 protection).

- Keeps the money collected on your behalf in a trust or escrow account.

- Turns the money over to you in a timely way. Some agencies do so on a monthly basis; others may remit funds to you every two weeks. Even better, some arrange for payments to go directly to you (rather than to the agency).

- Abides by a code of ethics. This code isn't fixed by state law; it is created by collection agency associations as a guideline for agency actions. However, it includes following federal and state law on fair collection practices, such as not harassing debtors.

Cost

It isn't cheap to work with a collection agency. An agency typically charges a percentage of whatever is recovered. The percentage can vary greatly from company to company, depending on the size of the outstanding claim and sometimes on how long the claim has been outstanding. The percentage can range up to 50 percent.

RESOURCES

To locate a collection agency, you can check out associations that agencies belong to (just recognize that membership is dependent only on the payment of a fee and is no assurance of competence):

- ACA International: The Association of Credit and Collection Professionals (www.acainternational.org and click on "Member Directory").

- Commercial Collection Agency Association (www.ccaa collect.com and click on "Member Directory" to search by state).

Legal Alternatives

You have two main legal avenues for collections: have an attorney try to collect on your behalf or do it yourself by suing in small-claims court.

Attorneys as Collectors

Instead of using a standard collection agency, you can hire an attorney who specializes in this area of law. These attorneys claim to be more successful than regular collection agencies, although they charge more for their services.

RESOURCES

To find attorneys who handle collections, do an Internet search for "collections attorneys." Also check Martindale.com, an attorney search engine, under "Location/Area of Practice" and then "Commercial Law" (www.martindale.com).

Suing to collect on past-due accounts is always a last resort. It can be a time-consuming and costly process, with no guarantee that even if you obtain a judgment you will actually be able to collect it. But if the amount outstanding is substantial or you simply feel it's a matter of principle, you may want to tell it to the judge.

To save money on attorneys' fees, consider handling the matter yourself through a small-claims court. In some small-claims courts as many as 60 percent of all cases are brought by small businesses. Usually, this is an expeditious process, allowing claims to be heard within a month or two. You don't need a lawyer, and court filing fees are minimal.

The rules for small-claims court vary from state to state. Each state has its own limits on how much you can sue for (if your claim is over this amount, you cannot use the small-claims process) and whether you can be subject to a counterclaim by the person you are suing. Also, some states limit the ability of corporations, no matter how small, to use the small-claims format. Some states permit you to use an attorney if you want to. And rules differ on how to serve the other party in order to start the action, with many states allowing service to be made easily by certified or registered mail.

Table 6.1 is a state-by-state chart of the key rules for small-claims court.

RESOURCES

For more details on small-claims court rules, connect to your state from www.consumeraffairs.com (click on "Small Claims Guide," then "State-by-state guide"). Also get help in collecting successful judgments at www.small-claims-court.net.

How to Proceed

If you decide to pursue the matter in court, ask the court clerk for the forms you need to start the action. Find out how to serve the other party (e.g., by certified or registered mail or with a process server or sheriff).

Make sure you observe all the time limits for action—when to serve, when to request evidence ("discovery") if permitted, and when to appear. Also be clear that you have not missed the deadline for starting an action. Generally, there is a statute of limitations, a period within which you have to commence your claim. This may be two years, four years, or some other time from the date of sale to start an action for collection. If you miss this deadline by even one day, you're too late and totally out of luck.

Make sure to take your claim to the right court. If you work across state lines, you usually have to bring your case to the small-claims court in the state in which your customer is based, which

TABLE 6.1 State-by-State Chart of Key Rules for Small-Claims Court

State	Claims Limitation and Other Rules
ALABAMA	
Maximum claim	$3,000
Attorneys	Allowed
Other	Equitable relief permitted
ALASKA	
Maximum claim	$10,000
Attorneys	Allowed
Other	Equitable relief permitted
ARIZONA	
Maximum claim	$2,500
Attorneys	Only if both parties agree in writing
Other	Equitable relief permitted
ARKANSAS	
Maximum claim	$5,000
Attorneys	Not allowed
Other	Corporations limited to 12 claims/year
CALIFORNIA	
Maximum claim	$5,000 (but no more than 2 claims over $2,500/year)
Attorneys	Not allowed
Other	Equitable relief available
COLORADO	
Maximum claim	$7,500
Attorneys	Not allowed (unless attorney is your full-time employee)
Other	No equitable relief (except nullification of contracts); limit 2 claims/month or 18/year
CONNECTICUT	
Maximum claim	$3,500
Attorneys	Allowed (required for corporations)
Other	No equitable relief

TABLE 6.1   *(Continued)*

State	Claims Limitation and Other Rules
DELAWARE (State does not have a small-claims court; small claims are heard by a justice of the peace)	
Maximum claim	$15,000
Attorneys	Allowed
DISTRICT OF COLUMBIA	
Maximum claim	$5,000
Attorneys	Allowed (required for corporations)
Other	No equitable relief
FLORIDA	
Maximum claim	$5,000
Attorneys	Allowed
Other	Equitable relief available
GEORGIA (State does not have a small-claims court; small claims are heard in magistrate court)	
Maximum claim	$15,000
Attorneys	Allowed
Other	Equitable relief available
HAWAII	
Maximum claim	$3,500
Attorneys	Allowed
Other	No equitable relief allowed
IDAHO	
Maximum claim	$4,000
Attorneys	Not allowed
Other	No punitive damages
ILLINOIS	
Maximum claim	$5,000 ($1,500 Cook County pro se)
Attorneys	Allowed (except Cook County pro se); required for corporations
Other	Court may order installment payments and/or arbitration

(Continued)

TABLE 6.1   *(Continued)*

State	Claims Limitation and Other Rules
INDIANA	
Maximum claim	$6,000
Attorneys	Allowed
Other	No equitable relief; court may order installment payments
IOWA	
Maximum claim	$4,000
Attorneys	Allowed
Other	No equitable relief; court may order installment payments
KANSAS	
Maximum claim	$1,800
Attorneys	Generally not allowed
KENTUCKY	
Maximum claim	$1,500
Attorneys	Allowed
Other	Limited equitable relief
LOUISIANA	
Maximum claim	$3,000
Attorneys	Allowed
Other	Equitable relief available; court may order installment payments
MAINE	
Maximum claim	$4,500
Attorneys	Allowed
Other	No equitable relief
MARYLAND	
Maximum claim	$5,000
Attorneys	Allowed
Other	No equitable relief
MASSACHUSETTS	
Maximum claim	$2,000
Attorneys	Allowed
Other	Mediation if both sides agree

TABLE 6.1 *(Continued)*

State	Claims Limitation and Other Rules
MICHIGAN	
Maximum claim	$3,000
Attorneys	Not allowed
Other	No equitable relief; court may refer case to mediation or arbitration
MINNESOTA	
Maximum claim	$7,000
Attorneys	Not allowed without court's permission (required for corporations)
Other	Court may order installment payments
MISSISSIPPI	
Maximum claim	$2,500
Attorneys	Allowed
Other	Some help in collecting judgments provided
MISSOURI	
Maximum claim	$3,000
Attorneys	Allowed
MONTANA	
Maximum claim	$3,000
Attorneys	Not allowed unless both sides represented
Other	Limit of 10 claims/year
NEBRASKA	
Maximum claim	$2,400 (adjusted every 5 years for inflation)
Attorneys	Not allowed
Other	Equitable relief available; limit of 2 claims/week (total 10 claims/year)
NEVADA	
Maximum claim	$5,000
Attorneys	Allowed
Other	No equitable relief

(Continued)

TABLE 6.1 *(Continued)*

State	Claims Limitation and Other Rules
NEW HAMPSHIRE	
Maximum claim	$5,000
Attorney	Allowed
NEW JERSEY	
Maximum claim	$2,000
Attorney	Allowed
NEW MEXICO	
Maximum claim	$10,000
Attorneys	Allowed (required for corporations)
Other	Voluntary mediation available
NEW YORK (Small-claims cases in New York City are heard in city civil court; in Nassau and Suffolk Counties in district court, except 1st District; in other cities in city court; in rural areas, in justice court)	
Maximum claim	$3,000
Attorneys	Allowed (required for most corporations)
Other	No equitable relief; business judgment debtors must pay within 35 days or $100 may be added to judgment (businesses that fail to pay judgments may face a refusal of renewal of grant of business license from authorities).
NORTH CAROLINA	
Maximum claim	$5,000
Attorneys	Allowed
Other	No equitable relief except enforcement of liens
NORTH DAKOTA	
Maximum claim	$5,000
Attorneys	Allowed
Other	No equitable relief

TABLE 6.1 *(Continued)*

State	Claims Limitation and Other Rules
OHIO	
Maximum claim	$3,000
Attorneys	Allowed
Other	No equitable relief; court may order arbitration
OKLAHOMA	
Maximum claim	$6,000
Attorneys	Allowed (fees limited)
OREGON	
Maximum claim	$5,000
Attorneys	Not allowed unless court consents
Other	Cases may be referred to mediation or arbitration
PENNSYLVANIA (In Philadelphia, small-claims cases are heard in municipal court; elsewhere, in district or justice court)	
Maximum claim	$10,000 in Philadelphia; $8,000 elsewhere
Attorneys	Allowed (required for corporations)
Other	Court may order installment payments
RHODE ISLAND	
Maximum claim	$1,500
Attorneys	Allowed (required for corporations other than small/family corporations)
Other	Court may order installment payments
SOUTH CAROLINA	
Maximum claim	$7,500
Attorney	Allowed
SOUTH DAKOTA	
Maximum claim	$8,000
Attorneys	Allowed

(Continued)

TABLE 6.1 *(Continued)*

State	Claims Limitation and Other Rules
TENNESSEE	
Maximum claim	$15,000; in counties of more than 700,000 population, $25,000
Attorneys	Allowed
Other	Limited equitable relief
TEXAS	
Maximum claim	$5,000
Attorneys	Allowed
Other	No equitable relief
UTAH	
Maximum claim	$5,000
Attorneys	Allowed
VERMONT	
Maximum claim	$3,500
Attorneys	Allowed
Other	No equitable relief
VIRGINIA	
Maximum claim	$1,000
Attorneys	Not allowed
WASHINGTON	
Maximum claim	$4,000
Attorneys	Not allowed unless court consents
Other	No equitable relief
WEST VIRGINIA	
Maximum claim	$5,000
Attorneys	Allowed
Other	No equitable relief
WISCONSIN	
Maximum claim	$5,000
Attorneys	Allowed
WYOMING	
Maximum claim	$3,000
Attorneys	Allowed
Other	Arbitration available in some circumstances

Note: Equitable relief means an award that is other than money (e.g., ordering the party to do or not do something).

may be different from your state. For example, a photographer based in Fairfield County, Connecticut, sued her customer located in Westchester County, New York, when he failed to pay for bar mitzvah photos, although she had to go to New York's small-claims court.

Impact of Winning Your Claim

Just because a court agrees that you're entitled to payment doesn't guarantee that you'll be any more successful in your collection efforts than you were prior to the lawsuit. You may have won a moral victory but are no closer to collecting money than before the suit. If there are no assets or wages to attach, your judgment may be worthless. Here are some key points to remember about life *after* you win a judgment:

- There may be a right of appeal (but if the other party doesn't do so within a set limit, such as 30 days, no appeal can be made).

- You have a long time in which to collect on the judgment, as fixed by state law (e.g., California has a 10-year limitation on collecting a judgment, with a 10-year renewal option). A party that doesn't have the funds to pay now may be in a better financial position to pay you later.

- State law allows interest to accrue on unpaid judgments (e.g., 6 percent or 8 percent; 10 percent per year in Hawaii), so the longer it goes unpaid, the more that is owed to you.

- The judgment stays on the other party's credit history for seven years. The party may have incentive to pay up so that satisfaction of the judgment is also noted on the credit report.

Retain an Attorney

If the amount that is owed is significant to you and is more than the small-claims limit, consider using an attorney who can handle your case on a contingency basis. Generally, you pay the attorney 33 percent to 40 percent of the recovery, plus court costs and other fees.

You can find an attorney specializing in collections through a collection agency. You can also find a collections attorney through the Columbia Law List at www.columbialist.com.

LESSONS ON COLLECTIONS

✔ Understand the importance of collections to your business.

✔ Check your customer's credit history before extending payment terms.

✔ Adopt smart invoicing policies.

✔ Offer customers different payment options for their convenience.

✔ Use creative collection strategies to get slow-paying customers to pay up.

✔ Use collection agencies when your efforts fail.

✔ Sue delinquent customers in small-claims court.

✔ Assess your other legal options.

Build and Maintain Credit and Restructure Debt

Out of debt, out of danger.

—Proverb

*C*ommerce today is long past the point of cash-and-carry; it runs to a large extent on credit. Your ability to buy on credit—through credit cards, installment agreements, or loans—is key to your business success. Bluntly put, without credit, your business probably can't make it.

Credit, like your good name, is something you earn and maintain. As a small-business owner, you need to be concerned about your personal credit rating as well as the credit standing of the business. Both affect your ability to borrow money and conduct business.

Sometimes, despite your best efforts, things happen that undermine your ability to repay your obligations. You fall behind, for whatever reason, and have creditors pounding on your door. When this happens, you face a crossroads: Choosing one path means you'll close your doors and go out of business; going the other way requires you to restructure your debts to pay off your creditors.

In this chapter you'll learn how to establish and use credit wisely. This means creating and maintaining a good credit history for both the business and you personally. It also means obtaining the best credit card for use in your business and using this credit sensibly.

You'll also see how, if problems arise, you can continue in business by making arrangements with creditors to pay them back—either over longer periods of time or for less than you owe them or a combination of both. You may be able to do this yourself or with the help of a commercial-debt-restructuring firm. If all else fails, you may need to seek bankruptcy protection, which can provide court supervision to pay off your debts over time.

Importance of a Credit Rating

Your word may be your bond, but your credit rating is what lenders, suppliers, and other people will use to decide whether to do business with you. You need to have good credit in order to get a loan, a line of credit, a business credit card, equipment leases, auto leases, and real estate mortgages if and when you need them.

And, even if another company does do business with you, your credit rating may affect the cost of doing business. For example, a company with a marginal credit rating may be able to obtain a loan, but it probably will have to pay a much higher annual percentage rate (APR) than a company that has a good credit rating.

A credit rating is a score developed by credit reporting companies to assess the likelihood that you'll pay back what you owe. The higher your score, the better credit risk you are deemed to be.

For your business, you have to be concerned with two credit ratings: the one for the business itself and your personal credit rating. In many situations, because you are a small-business owner, your personal score can be the deciding factor in whether your business can obtain financing.

Establishing and Fixing Personal Credit

Personal credit is based on a number of factors, including your outstanding debt balance on personal credit cards, the number of lines of open credit accounts you have (even if they are not drawn upon), and your bill payment history (e.g., if and how many times you have been more than 30 days late in paying an outstanding bill). Your personal credit is expressed in terms of a FICO score, which is a number assigned by Fair Isaac Corporation, a credit rating bureau, to reflect your credit history. The number usually ranges from 300 to 900; the higher the number, the better your score.

Establishing Credit

The way to establish credit is to use credit and do so wisely. If you do not have any credit cards, your credit history is so thin that it can't be said whether you have a good or bad rating. Credit ratings also take into account the promptness of your payments on utilities bills, car finance arrangements, and rent or mortgage payments.

Repairing a Bad Credit Report

Personal credit ratings are set by the three major credit reporting bureaus:

1. Equifax (www.equifax.com)

2. Experian (www.experian.com)

3. TransUnion (www.transunion.com)

Under the Fair and Accurate Credit Transactions Act (FACTA), you are now entitled to a free credit report annually. As of September 1, 2005, you can do so regardless of the state in which you live.

RESOURCES

To obtain your free annual report, contact Central Source (a site sponsored by the three major credit bureaus) at (877) FACTACT or go to www.annualcreditreport.com.

Check your report carefully to make sure everything is correct. If there are errors—such as old loans still being reported or unpaid items that aren't yours (they belong to the other Mr. Jones)—get them corrected. A landscaper in Oregon had his credit rating damaged because of a name mix-up, a problem he discovered when he was turned down for a business credit card. Talk with your credit bureau to find out what documentation is needed to update your files. It may be as simple as your writing a letter requesting the correction.

In writing the letter, include all the essential information pertaining to the nature of the error and how it should be corrected. Do not add more since credit reporting bureaus receive 10,000 letters each day. Send your letter, along with any proof that what is being reported is not true (e.g., a canceled check showing that you made a payment reported as unpaid on your credit report), by certified mail so you have proof of mailing. Retain a copy of everything you send in case you need to resubmit information.

Establishing and Fixing Business Credit

Like your personal credit standing, your business can establish and build a good credit report. Your business credit is separate from your personal credit. Credit in your company name is tied to your federal tax identification number (your employer identification number that you obtain from the IRS).

Use this number when opening a business bank account and applying for a credit card in the company name. This will then build up credit under the business name.

Establishing Credit

While a personal credit rating is generally based on credit card debt and other bills, a commercial credit rating is tied more closely to bill paying to suppliers and for lines of credit. Banks, suppliers, and other businesses that work with you can obtain a credit report showing the status of your business from credit reporting agencies such as Dun & Bradstreet (D&B) (www.dnb.com). D&B has developed a PAYDEX score based on your bill-paying experience over the past year (only vendors that report to D&B are factored into the score). Other businesses can use the score in assessing whether you seem creditworthy—the higher the score, the more likely you are to pay your bills. A score of 70 or above enables you to more easily obtain credit and extended payment terms. (See Table 7.1.) To keep your score as high as possible, be sure to pay large vendors (which are likely to report to D&B) ahead of smaller vendors when you are in a cash crunch.

Equifax Small Business Enterprise provides a small business credit report to help other companies, from banks to utilities com-

TABLE 7.1   PAYDEX Score Ratings

PAYDEX Score	Payment
100	Anticipate
90	Discount
80	Prompt
70	15 days beyond terms
60	22 days beyond terms
50	30 days beyond terms
40	60 days beyond terms
30	90 days beyond terms
20	120 days beyond terms
UN	Unavailable

panies and suppliers, decide whether to do business with you. See (www.equifax.com/sitePages/biz/smallBiz and click on "Grant Credit").

It usually takes several years to build up business credit, so start to do so as soon as your business commences operations. Take advantage of increased access to credit, such as a line of credit from your business credit card, to continue building up a favorable credit history.

Repairing Credit

If your company experiences cash flow problems, you're bound to have repayment difficulties that will result in damage to your credit report. There is no avoiding this result. Your aim should be repairing the damage as quickly as possible. Since the credit report is primarily a snapshot of the past year, work to pay bills as promptly as possible so that as each month goes by your report looks better and better.

Using Business Credit Cards

For small businesses, credit cards often are a lifeline, providing credit when it is needed most. Despite high interest rates, most entrepreneurs start up businesses on personal credit cards because it is the only way for them to obtain financing. Hopefully, as your business becomes established, you can apply for and use business credit cards based on the company's credit rating. (Business credit cards are referred to as "corporate cards" even if your business isn't a corporation.)

Of course, when credit cards are used as a financing tool, they become costly. To keep costs down, apply for and use only those business credit cards that provide attractive terms for your business. Points to keep in mind when comparison shopping for these cards:

- Look for no or low annual fees.

- Check the interest rate that will be charged on outstanding balances *after* the initial introductory rate (which may be 0 percent for the first six months you have the card).

- Review the line of credit that the card entitles you to (e.g., $20,000). Your line of credit is the amount of goods and services you can charge on the card. You may also have a credit limit on the card for cash advances; this may be lower than the general line of credit for making purchases.

- Consider rebate cards—those that give you money back or credit toward other purchases based on what you buy (rebates on gasoline, frequent-flier miles, etc.).

RESOURCES

Some business credit cards with attractive terms include:

- Advanta (www.advanta.com) has a number of different business credit cards that offer not only benefits but also detailed expense management reports to track your business spending. Card types include:
  - Advanta Platinum Business MasterCard, which offers credit lines up to $100,000 and 0 percent APR on balance transfers for the first nine months.

- Advanta Cash Back Business Credit Card, with 2 percent rebates on all business purchases and credit lines up to $100,000.

- Advanta Bonus Miles Business Credit Card, which can be used to earn points toward airline ticket purchases (without any blackout periods).

- Advanta Gas Reward Platinum Business Credit Card, which gives you 3 percent back on gasoline purchases.

- Blue for Business from OPEN: The Small Business Network (www.americanexpress.com/cardfinder/apply.cgi? 46/840/b/9) offers a 0 percent introductory rate for the first nine months (and rates as low as 9.99 percent thereafter). Cardholders can enjoy discounts at FedEx, Hertz, Hilton Hotels, and more and may qualify for a line of credit up to $50,000.

- CapitalOne Visa Business Platinum Card (www.capitalone .com and click on "Small Business") lets you personalize your card with your company name, add cards for employees at no cost, and obtain a fixed APR of 8.9 percent, with a credit limit up to $20,000.

- Chase-BankOne Visa Platinum Business Card (www .bankone.com and click on "Business") offers 0 percent APR for five months, with a credit limit up to $35,000.

Maintaining Good Credit

Like acquiring a good credit rating for your business, the way in which to keep a good credit rating is to repay your debts in a timely manner. This means paying outstanding bills in the time allotted. Creditors who are paid late can and often do report your tardiness to reporting bureaus, which negatively impacts your credit rating.

Facing Unmanageable Debt

Just about every business faces difficult financial periods at some time. Despite the best of business plans, tough times can result from things beyond your control, such as weather-related catastrophes like Hurricane Katrina, problems with suppliers, or other unexpected events. Business credit cards and other financing options you've put in place may not pull you through. Whatever the cause of the difficulties, it is up to you to pay your creditors or go out of business.

Recognize the Problem

If you face a growing inability to pay your bills when they come due, you may have serious cash flow problems (see Chapter 5). These can be the result of:

- *Lack of sales*. You're not bringing in the dollars you need to cover your expenses.

- *Slow or uncollectible receivables*. You've made sales, but aren't receiving payment on a timely basis.

- *Undercapitalization*. You don't have enough money on hand to carry you through a period of tight cash flow.

If you become like some of your customers and are behind in paying your bills, recognize that you have a problem. It won't help to duck the issue and hope for a better tomorrow. You may already be afraid to answer the phone for fear that creditors are demanding immediate and full payment. You must take action to avoid further problems.

Consider the Alternatives

Your creditors are at the door, demanding payment and threatening to sue you. What can you do?

First assess where you stand. Is the problem serious? Temporary? Are you personally responsible for your company's debts (you gave your personal guarantee, such as on a bank loan to your company or a commercial lease)? Are there outstanding tax obligations for which you are personally liable, which includes income tax withholding and the employees' share of Social Security and Medicare taxes? Are there other obligations for which you are personally liable (e.g., employees' salaries)?

Second, understand what happens when you don't pay your creditors. They can't just waltz through your doors and take your computers off your desks or tools out of your cabinets, or seize your business bank account. But they can if they sue you and obtain a judgment. They can even force you into bankruptcy where you could be required to liquidate your company's assets and distribute the proceeds to the creditors, keeping nothing, not even a going business.

Assuming the problem isn't a temporary cash flow issue, you can try to restructure your debts yourself by approaching your creditors. Some creditors will oblige, giving you more time to repay or easing the credit terms. This tactic can be especially useful when dealing with companies you've done business with for a long time. But you may find some creditors who are not willing to work with you—because they don't trust you (e.g., you've made promises that weren't kept) or for any other reason (e.g., they're in a cash crunch and can't wait for your slower repayment).

Then you face serious choices. You can shut your doors and go out of business. However, this may be more difficult than it sounds. If you are a sole proprietor or a general partner in a partnership, closing the business won't relieve you of your obligation to pay the business's outstanding debts; you remain personally liable for business debts. And even if the business is a limited liability company or corporation, which ordinarily gives you legal protection against personal liability, you may have personally guaranteed some debts of the business. In this case, even though the business is closed, you remain personally obligated to make good on your guarantee.

You can seek bankruptcy protection. Under Chapter 11 of the U.S. Bankruptcy Code, you can gain court protection to reorganize (see later in this chapter). This means you continue operations while working out a repayment plan with your creditors that is overseen by a court. The main problem with this alternative is cost; attorneys' fees on reorganization plans can be pricey.

You can use a debt restructuring service to create a plan to get out of debt. Typically, these services will work with small businesses that have debts of at least $15,000 and a minimum number of creditors (e.g., four) and can afford to make monthly payments of at least 2 percent of the amount they owe per month. Creditors may be willing to work with an intermediary—a commercial debt restructuring firm—because there is a third party assuring them of repayment, whereas they might not have been amenable to your direct proposals.

Restructuring Debt

Consumers who face mounting personal debt can turn to any number of credit counseling services. These services, many of which are nonprofit agencies, create repayment plans and work with creditors to arrange terms that individuals can handle. Companies do not have the same range of options—there are no nonprofit agencies that specialize in helping small businesses get out of debt.

There are, however, companies that can help a business reach agreements with creditors to pay over time and avoid the need for a court-supervised repayment plan under the bankruptcy law. For example, Commercial Credit Counseling Services, Inc. (www.saveyourcompany.com) provides solutions for troubled small businesses. The company acts as an intermediary between you and your creditors to develop a plan that you can afford and creditors will accept. The company's fee for its plan is built into the payments, so that debtors do not pay any more than they would have if they'd made full payment on their outstanding debts.

There are other commercial-debt-restructuring companies that you can find through the World Wide Web. And it is always a good idea to check with your local Better Business Bureau before doing business with any firm.

Benefits of Restructuring to the Debtor

A repayment plan allows a company to avoid a liquidation and stay in business. Other benefits:

- Using a debt-restructuring firm lifts the burden—both psychological and time—from the business owner of having to deal with creditors, collection agencies, and creditors' attorneys. Collection calls can stop, leaving more time for the business owner to devote to running the business.

- A repayment plan can help prevent a debtor's bank account from being frozen, a move that could undermine the business's existence. One New Jersey furnace sales company that had been in business for more than 25 years but fell upon hard times was about to have its heat turned off, but restructuring forestalled this dire event.

- Sticking to a repayment schedule can have a positive effect on your company's credit rating, even though you are in the midst of a repayment plan. As mentioned earlier, the sooner you start making timely payments, the sooner you can establish a favorable credit rating.

How Restructuring Works

In order to develop a repayment plan, a small business must determine its problem creditors—the creditors it cannot afford to pay. The amounts owed are verified by the creditor. The debt-restructuring company then creates a plan, based on the debtor's budget and the creditor's cooperation. Some creditors may accept less than full payment in order to receive money quickly, cutting the amount of your outstanding debt. Other creditors can receive full payment if they are willing to wait. The restructuring plan may take weeks to create but years to complete (on average, repayment plans run from 15 to 40 months). Typically, monthly payments are fixed at 2 percent to 3 percent of the outstanding debt, so that if you owe a total of $100,000, expect to pay $2,500 (2.5 percent) each month under a debt-restructuring plan.

You can select the creditors with whom you wish to enter into a restructuring plan, leaving your critical suppliers out of the loop (provided that you can pay them in full when due).

Note: For farmers and ranchers, the U.S. Department of Agriculture's Farm Service Agency provides credit counseling and advice (www.fsa.usda.gov/pas and search "credit counseling" for access to local offices of the agency).

Bankruptcy as a Last Resort

If you can't restructure your debts on your own (or with the help of a debt-restructuring firm), you may be forced to turn to bankruptcy protection if you want to stay in business. Filing for protection under Chapter 11 of the U.S. Bankruptcy Code gives you a temporary reprieve—once you file a petition, your creditors have to back off and give you time to work out a repayment plan. (Family farms and commercial fishermen have special reorganization rules under Chapter 12 of the code.) Your creditors may be willing to settle for less than full repayment because the plan is monitored by a court so that they are virtually assured of their settlement amount.

How Bankruptcy Works

You file a petition in a U.S. bankruptcy court, indicating that you are opting under Chapter 11 for a plan of reorganization. You can also elect to be treated as a small business if eligible to do so (see next subsection). You then become what is called a "debtor in possession" because you retain control of your assets and running your business. Generally no trustee is appointed by the court to take control of your assets and your business. You remain in this status until either your case is dismissed, it is converted to a Chapter 7 bankruptcy liquidation (where assets are sold off and the business is completely shut down), or a trustee is appointed.

All of your creditors must be notified in accordance with bankruptcy rules about your filing for protection (you cannot pick and choose creditors as you can with your own debt restructuring). Then a committee is formed to develop your repayment plan. The committee is made up of some creditors and you. Once the plan is created, it must be "confirmed" (approved) by the court. You then have to live by the terms you've agreed to, making timely payments to your creditors as dictated by the plan.

Special Rules for Small Businesses

Small businesses, defined as those with unsecured and secured debts of under $2 million (unsecured debts are ordinary obligations owed to suppliers; secured debts are collateralized loans), can now use an expedited procedure to pass through bankruptcy and continue operations. (In the past there had been a $4 million cap on single-asset real estate cases that prevented otherwise "small" businesses from using expedited procedures.) A plan of reorganization usually must be filed within 180 days of the bankruptcy petition. Then a court generally must confirm the plan of reorganization within 45 days of submission. Under the Bankruptcy Abuse Prevention and Consumer Protection Act of 2005, which took effect on October 17, 2005, new standardized forms should make it somewhat easier to give required notification to creditors, which may save a small business both time and money.

Drawbacks to Bankruptcy

While bankruptcy protection may sound good at first blush, understand the drawbacks:

- The process is costly because of attorneys' fees involved (you can't do it yourself).

- You are under court supervision. You are required, for example, to submit certain periodic reports to the government regarding profitability, cash flow, and whether taxes are being paid on time.

- You may not avoid all of your debts. For example, most tax debts are nondischargable—you cannot get out of paying them even if you use a reorganization plan.

RESOURCES

To find an attorney who can assist you in the bankruptcy process, go to Bankruptcy Law Firms.com at www.bankruptcy lawfirms.com.

LESSONS ON BUILDING UP CREDIT AND RESTRUCTURING DEBT

✔ Understand the importance to your company of having good credit.

✔ Repair your personal credit if necessary.

✔ Establish good credit for your business, separate and apart from your personal credit.

✔ Find the right credit card for your business to help build up your company's credit.

✔ Keep your credit rating high by paying bills in a timely manner.

✔ Use a debt-restructuring firm to help you work out repayment terms with creditors when you face unmanageable repayment obligations.

✔ Use bankruptcy only as a last resort to settle with creditors and stay in business.

Meet Your Tax Obligations

One of the major characteristics of our tax system, and one in which we can take a great deal of pride, is that it operates primarily through individual self-assessment.

—John F. Kennedy

When you have a job, your tax obligations are basically limited to paying your income taxes each year. And meeting that liability is simplified by having taxes withheld from each paycheck to satisfy your annual tax liability. But when you run a business, you face tax obligations of various types every day. You have to be concerned not only with income tax on your business profits, but also with employment taxes for your staff and sales tax on the goods and services you sell. There may also be excise taxes and use taxes to be paid, as well as various information returns to be filed with the government. The burden on business owners is twofold: the amount of tax you owe, which reduces the money you can keep from your efforts, and the paperwork to keep necessary records and file required returns, which reduces the time you have to spend directly on making money from your business. If you pay someone else to do it, then it further reduces what you can keep.

But no matter how onerous this burden may be, you cannot escape it. Face it—taxes are an inevitable cost of doing business. The taxes you pay are the difference between what you earn and what you keep, so the more you can lower your taxes, the more you retain. But whether you prepare *returns yourself, have them done by an in-house tax person, or use an outside accountant, there's time and cost involved.*

The failure to meet your tax obligations can undermine your business and, in some cases, result in government seizure of your business assets or personal liability for your company's tax bill. You may have walked down the main street in your city or town only to see a storefront closed up with a notice on the door saying "Closed for sales taxes."

In this chapter you will learn what tax obligations you face as a business owner. Each type of tax has its own set of rules and obligations for making tax payments and filing returns. You'll also find out about ways to help you meet these obligations and, where possible, simplify your responsibilities.

Tax Obligations in General

Taxes are the revenue that the government uses to provide goods and services. There is usually no correlation between the amount of taxes you pay and what you receive from the government. In fact, the better you do, the more you'll pay, usually without deriving any direct benefit. Still, taxes are a fixed and certain cost of doing business.

There is, of course, a huge underground economy, estimated in March 2005 at somewhere around $200 billion (no one knows for sure). This underground economy includes businesses that fail to report income and do not pay taxes they owe. Much of the unreported income is from illegal activities, such as drug trafficking and illegal gambling. But many hardworking small-business owners in cash businesses are part of the underground economy.

Obviously, there are valid reasons why businesses should meet their tax obligations. First, failing to do so is against the law and can result in civil and even criminal penalties. While it is true that many get away with underreporting income, don't think that this is any guarantee you won't be one of the ones who gets caught. The IRS is increasingly sophisticated in its examination tactics. For instance, there are currently more than three dozen audit guides telling agents what to look for when examining certain types of businesses, from auto body shops to veterinarians, and more guides are being added.

For example, when examining pizzerias, the audit guide instructs agents to look at deductions for purchases of flour in order to deduce the number of pizzas that have been made and sold by the establishment. If flour purchases greatly outnumber the amount needed for the pizza sales reported, then the government knows that underreporting is taking place. To view IRS audit guides, go to www.irs.gov and search for "audit techniques guides."

Second, not reporting income can adversely affect business owners personally. For example, say a person in a cash business reports only $20,000 of income for the year when he is really netting over $100,000. When he wants to buy a home with a mortgage, some lenders base loans on reported income ($20,000), even though the business owner's lifestyle is more in keeping with actual income ($100,000). He may lose out on the home he wants and can afford because he has not reported all of his income.

Third, there is the worry factor. The IRS is always on the lookout for tax cheats, and this may keep you up at night. An IRS audit can happen, for example, when a disgruntled employee who knows about unreported income tells the IRS about the company in hopes of receiving a reward. It can also occur as part of an IRS audit program. For example, at the end of 2005, the IRS was set to audit 5,000 randomly selected S corporation returns for tax years 2003 and 2004 as part of an audit program. The program was being used to develop better audit techniques so that the IRS could more effectively select and examine S corporation returns in the future.

Working with Tax Professionals

Because of the continual changes in the tax rules, it is virtually impossible for a business owner to run the company *and* keep current on taxes. The IRS estimates that about 80 percent of small-business owners use tax professionals to prepare their returns.

Whether you choose to use a professional or do it yourself is entirely up to you; it depends on your level of expertise in taxes and the amount of time you have to devote to this activity. Fortunately, today there are a number of software programs that can help small-business owners handle various tax chores, such as filing income tax returns and preparing Forms 1099-MISC for independent contractors.

But whether you work with a tax professional or handle your own taxes, recognize that you—not the professional—are liable for taxes and responsible for all filings and payments. If your professional makes an error, you may have a case against him or her for malpractice, but you remain liable to the government for tax underpayments, nonpayments, and nonfilings.

Choosing the right tax professional for your situation is discussed in Chapter 3.

Income Tax Returns

If your business is profitable, you probably are liable for income taxes. Whether this obligation is imposed on you or on the company depends on how the company is organized. If you are a self-employed individual or an owner in a pass-through entity—a partnership, a limited liability company (LLC), or an S corporation—you owe income taxes on your share of business profit. C corporations are separate taxpaying entities. C corporations pay tax on their profits; shareholders in these corporations pay tax on only distributions to them, such as salary and dividends.

You may owe taxes to the federal government as well as to the state (or states) in which you do business. The rules on income taxes may vary between the federal government and the states.

Your Obligation

As the owner of a business, you have a responsibility to see that the company files a tax return. A return is required whether the business makes or loses money. It must be filed each year, even if no tax is due. The return you use for federal income taxes depends on your type of entity, as shown in Table 8.1.

If there is more than one owner of a business, how is this responsibility shared?

- *Partnerships.* All general partners are obligated to file the partnership return. However, only one general partner has to sign the return. Usually this is the tax matters partner (TMP), a person named by the partnership on the return to represent the business in tax matters before the IRS. But smaller partnerships

TABLE 8.1   Federal Income Tax Returns for Businesses

Sole proprietor, independent contractor, or one-member LLC*	Schedule C (or a simplified Schedule C-EZ) of Form 1040
Partnership or LLC*	Form 1065
S corporation	Form 1120S
C corporation	Form 1120

*Assuming the LLC has not elected to be taxed as a corporation.

(those with 10 or fewer partners) may not have a TMP, so any general partner can sign the return in this case.

- *Limited liability companies.* The member-manager or, if there is no member-manager, then all members are obligated to file the partnership return for the LLC. However, this obligation has not yet been made clear by the IRS. Only one member has to sign the return. If there is a member-manager, this person usually is the signer.

- *S corporations.* The return must be filed and signed by either the president, vice president, treasurer, assistant treasurer, chief accounting officer, or any other corporate officer authorized to sign the return. These individuals need not be shareholders, although in most small S corporations the shareholders are also the corporate officers.

- *C corporations.* The return must be filed and signed by either the president, vice president, treasurer, assistant treasurer, chief accounting officer, or any other corporate officer authorized to sign the return. These individuals need not be shareholders, although in most small corporations the shareholders are also the corporate officers.

Then, if you are a sole proprietor or an owner of a pass-through entity, you file your personal income tax returns to report your share of business income or loss. In effect, you have to file two returns. For example, say you are the sole shareholder of an S corporation and act as the corporate president. You must file the S corporation return. You must also report all of the S corporation income on your personal income tax return.

State Income Taxes

In addition to federal income taxes, there may also be state income tax obligations. Your responsibility to file a state tax return and pay state income taxes does not depend on where the business is set up, but rather on where you do business. For instance, if you incorporated in Delaware but operate solely in Illinois, you owe income taxes to Illinois (you may also owe a tax or fee to Delaware).

Generally, doing business in a state means having a nexus (connection) to it. This is usually based on whether you have a physical presence within a state (e.g., maintaining an office or a sales force in a state). Just shipping goods into a state is generally not considered a nexus for state income tax purposes. The Business Activity Tax Simplification Act (BAT), a measure pending when this book went to press, would impose a federal (i.e., uniform) definition of nexus on the states.

If you have a business connection with more than one state, you owe income taxes to each one (assuming that each imposes a state income tax). Your profits are apportioned between or among the states in which you have a nexus. Apportionment is a highly complex process, based on a sales factor, a payroll factor, and a property factor.

Strategies for Income Taxes

Your objective with respect to income tax is to pay every penny owed but not one penny more. Minimizing taxes depends on your ability to take advantage of tax breaks, including various deductions, exemptions, and tax credits. This is not an easy task, given the ever-changing tax landscape. At the very least, review annual law changes listed in the IRS instructions to your return.

Another objective is to avoid a tax audit. If you are examined by the IRS or your state, it can be a costly and very time-consuming process that can severely cut into your ability to run your business. Here are some key ways to reduce the chances of being audited:

AVOID ANY RED FLAGS

Don't take any positions on the return that can alert the IRS to possible problems with your taxes. For example, if you are turning a hobby into a business and expect to experience losses in the start-up years, it may not be wise to rely on an IRS presumption that you are engaged in the activity to make a profit, a presumption that is claimed by filing IRS Form 5213, Election to Postpone Determination as to Whether the Presumption Applies That an Activity Is Engaged In for Profit. Filing this form automatically keeps the IRS at bay for five years (or seven years in the case of certain horse-related activities)—the presumption period—but virtually guarantees that the IRS will review prior returns at the end of these years. To avoid the near certainty of an examination, it may be preferable to take other measures to ensure that you can prove a profit motive if the IRS should arbitrarily select you for an audit. Unfortunately, there is no published list for red flags; ask your tax professional for some ideas here (although tax experts differ on what positions are red flags).

ERR ON THE SIDE OF CAUTION

When in doubt, take the more conservative alternative; it is usually less likely to draw IRS attention. And even if you are examined, you are more likely to win your position. For instance, when you engage a new worker in your business and are not certain whether to treat him or her as an employee or an independent contractor, opting for the more conservative position by designating the worker as an employee may be a less costly strategy in the long run. The IRS will never oppose this classification; the other choice could lead to costly wrangling with the IRS or your state.

FOLLOW IRS INSTRUCTIONS

Simple things, such as carefully completing returns and entering all required information, can avoid having the IRS take a closer look at your return.

KEEP GOOD BOOKS AND RECORDS

Be able to prove any positions you do take on returns. No matter how careful you are, there is always an audit risk. But having required receipts and other substantiation for deductions claimed on a return can minimize the effects if any examination should occur.

FILE ON TIME

File tax returns on time (including any filing extensions that may be obtained). Late-filed returns may receive greater scrutiny during processing. But returns filed after the due date pursuant to a filing extension do not necessarily get a closer look than returns filed by the original due date. For instance, those in disaster areas caused by Hurricane Katrina were given six-month extensions to file returns, make tax payments, and complete other tax chores due after August 29, 2004. And, for 2005 returns, all taxpayers—C corporations, sole proprietors, and owners of pass-through entities—can obtain an automatic six-month filing extension simply by filing for one no later than the due date of the return; no reason is necessary.

Estimated Taxes

Our income tax system operates on a pay-as-you-go basis. This is largely reflected in income tax withholding on wage earners. But businesses that are profitable must also pay a portion of their income taxes through the year by means of estimated tax payments.

C corporations make their own estimated tax payments for the corporate tax; sole proprietors and owners of pass-through entities pay personal estimated taxes. (S corporations become taxpayers and are liable for estimated taxes only in very limited situations not discussed here.)

Your Obligation

Estimated taxes are due quarterly if annual tax liability (above any tax prepayments) is expected to exceed $500 for C corporations and $1,000 for sole proprietors and owners of pass-through entities. For taxpayers on a calendar year, the due date for reporting estimated taxes is shown in Table 8.2.

Strategies for Meeting Your Obligation

Business owners who were formerly employees had met their personal tax obligation largely through wage withholding and may not

TABLE 8.2   Estimated Tax Due Dates for Calendar-Year Taxpayers*

	C Corporations	Individuals
First installment	April 15	April 15
Second installment	June 15	June 15
Third installment	September 15	September 15
Fourth installment	December 15	January 15 of following year

*Due date is extended to the next business day if the fixed date falls on a Saturday, Sunday, or legal holiday.

be accustomed to paying estimated taxes. Your unfamiliarity with estimated taxes can create two problems: (1) Remembering the estimated tax due dates throughout the year so as to avoid penalties and (2) having the cash on hand to make these tax payments.

To ensure that you don't overlook any estimated tax due date, you might want to use the Electronic Federal Tax Payment System (EFTPS). This is an online payment method in which you direct the transfer of funds from your bank account to the U.S. Treasury on set dates. You can schedule payments in advance—up to 365 days in advance for individuals or 180 days in advance for corporations. Businesses that had tax payments of $200,000 or more in 2004 are required to use EFTPS in 2006. Small businesses and their owners are not required to use EFTPS, but millions have already enrolled in the program for their own convenience. To learn more about EFTPS and enroll, go to www.eftps.gov.

To ensure that you have sufficient funds on hand to pay personal estimated taxes, it is highly advisable for small-business owners to set up a separate bank account and segregate funds for this purpose. Often money that flows into the business is needed for business or personal expenses, leaving little remaining for taxes. Make tax payments a priority and stash the cash needed for this obligation on a regular and systematic basis. For example, if you figure that estimated tax payments for the year will require installments of $3,000 each, then be sure to save $1,000 in a separate account each month so that you'll have the money to pay the tax bill.

Estimated taxes are not easy to figure because income and expenses of a business are usually not constant throughout the year.

You may have good or great months as well as fair or poor months. To escape penalty for underpayment, estimated taxes for sole proprietors and owners of pass-through entities for the year must turn out to be at least 90 percent of the actual liability for the year (over the $1,000 threshold mentioned earlier). Usually, this means dividing your annual projected tax liability by four and paying one-fourth each quarter. C corporations generally must pay 100 percent of the tax shown on the return for the current year.

If you want to better match your income with estimated tax payments, then use the annualization method, which helps you pay taxes in proportion to the income for the quarter. For instance, if you are a retailer and earn most of your money through holiday sales in the final quarter of the year, using the annualization method will minimize payments for the first three quarters but allow you to escape any estimate tax underpayments by boosting the final payment for the year.

For corporations there is also a special way to figure estimated taxes, called the adjusted seasonal method, which may be advisable for corporations with recurring seasonal income. This method takes into account income earned in the three preceding years.

You can also calculate estimated tax payments by basing installments on income from the prior year. To avoid penalties, make sure that your estimated tax payments for this year are at least 100 percent of the tax you paid in the prior year (special restrictions for large corporations limit the 100 percent prior year rule to the first installment of estimated taxes). For sole proprietors and owners of pass-through entities, if your adjusted gross income for the prior year was over $150,000, then you must pay at least 110 percent of the prior year's tax; corporations do not have this higher limit.

One of the problems for some business owners isn't figuring the amount of estimated tax due, but rather having the cash on hand to make a timely payment. A house painter in Chicago had his bank automatically transfer 25 percent of every deposit into a personal account so that he'd have the cash needed to make his estimated tax payments. An unincorporated dentist in Omaha, however, found the burden of making estimated taxes too troublesome. She incorporated her practice so that income tax withholding on her salary would cover a sizable portion of her tax payments due for the year.

For more information about estimated taxes, see the official instructions to IRS Form 2210, Underpayment of Estimated Tax by Individuals, Estates, and Trusts (for self-employed individuals and owners of pass-through entities), and IRS Form 2220, Underpayment of Estimated Tax by Corporations (for C corporations), as well as IRS Publication 505, *Tax Withholding and Estimated Tax*, which can be downloaded from the IRS web site (www.irs.gov).

Employment Taxes

If your company has one or more employees, you have employment tax obligations. This is true even if you are the only employee of your corporation.

Your Obligation

Tax responsibilities for employment taxes are numerous and include:

- Withholding income tax (federal and, where applicable, state) from employee wages.
- Withholding the employee share of Social Security and Medicare (FICA) taxes.
- Withholding state disability fund payments (in California, New Jersey, New York, Rhode Island, and West Virginia).
- Paying the employer share of Social Security and Medicare (FICA) taxes.
- Paying unemployment insurance tax (federal and state).
- Filing W-2 forms each year. This means furnishing copies to employees as well as providing all the forms to the Social Security Administration.
- Filing quarterly employer returns for income tax withholding and FICA with the IRS as well as quarterly state withholding forms (although the IRS is now consideriing annual returns for small employers).
- Filing annual employer returns for unemployment taxes with the IRS and the state.

- Depositing employment taxes according to IRS-set schedules or making tax payments with returns.

Aside from the big number of obligations, understanding the rules so that you can comply isn't easy. What wages are taxable? What fringe benefits are subject to tax? Which ones are exempt? As an employer you need to learn the answers to these questions so you can avoid tax problems.

Strategies for Meeting Your Obligation

Because of the burden of employment taxes, there is no easy fix. You can handle your obligations in-house, especially if you have a bookkeeper, accountant, or other designated tax person who understands the scope of the obligation. The IRS provides several free publications that can assist you in managing your employment taxes. You can download the following publications from www.irs.gov:

- IRS Publication 15, Circular E, *Employer's Tax Guide*, is the essential booklet for all employers. This guide explains the rules for employees, including family employees; withholding on tips and supplemental wages; and depositing taxes. It also contains income tax and FICA withholding tables.

- IRS Publication 15-A, *Employer's Supplemental Tax Guide*, helps you determine whether workers are employees or independent contractors. It also provides alternative methods for figuring withholding.

- IRS Publication 15-B, *Employer's Tax Guide to Fringe Benefits*, explains which benefits are taxable and which are exempt from income tax and/or FICA taxes.

Your state may also have one or more employment tax guides to assist you in meeting your state employment tax obligations.

Many small businesses work with payroll companies, such as Automatic Data Processing, Inc. (ADP) and PayChex. These companies can manage all of a business's payroll obligations, from figuring withholding and other taxes to providing W-2s and preparing employer returns. The more you have a payroll company handle for you, the more you'll pay for the service. But weigh the cost of the service against the savings you realize from having more time to devote to your business.

Still other small businesses let their outside accountants assist them in handling their payroll tax obligations. Again, you will pay for this service, but may find it well worth the cost.

Depositing Payroll Taxes

It is vital for small-business owners not only to understand the special nature of payroll taxes but also to pay them to the government on a timely basis. The law fixes the time when you must make payments of payroll taxes. Depending on the amount of taxes owed, you may have to make deposits on a monthly or semiweekly basis. If you are late, you are subject to penalties. The more quickly you remedy the problem, the smaller your penalties will be.

When it comes to the part of employment taxes that are employee tax payments—income tax withholding and the employee share of Social Security and Medicare taxes—you are merely an agent for your employees. These taxes, referred to as trust fund taxes, are sacred. You are 100 percent personally liable for the payment of these taxes, regardless of how your business is organized. For example, if you are a member of an LLC and choose to pay another creditor with the trust fund money that should have gone to Uncle Sam, you are personally liable to the IRS for these taxes. The personal liability protection of the LLC does not help you in this situation.

This personal responsibility usually extends to owners, officers, or other responsible persons. Even if there is more than one responsible person (e.g., two equal shareholders of an S corporation), the IRS can collect the entire tax from any responsible person. It is then up to the one who pays to try to collect a share from other responsible persons using the federal right of contribution, a legal right to collect a share from someone else who is responsible.

Information Returns

The IRS uses businesses as their agents to report certain activities so that the IRS knows what's going on. The government requires you to file an information return to report certain income or other activities. Here is a partial listing of the types of these information returns. All reporting is on an annual basis unless otherwise indicated:

- **Dividends.** If your corporation has paid out dividends of $10 or more to any person, including to you, report the amount of the dividends to the IRS and the recipient on IRS Form 1099-DIV, Dividends and Distributions.

- **Large cash transactions.** If you receive more than $10,000 in cash in one or more transactions in the course of your business, you must report the transaction to the IRS by the 15th day after the date the cash was received. For example, if you sell used cars and are paid $12,000 in cash for a pre-owned car, report this payment to the IRS. Reporting for large cash transactions is made on IRS Form 8300, Report of Cash Payments Over $10,000 Received in a Trade or Business.

- **Payments to independent contractors.** If you pay a total of $600 or more to a contractor, subcontractor, or freelancer in the year, report the amount to the IRS and the contractor on IRS Form 1099-MISC, Miscellaneous Income.

- **Pension and retirement plan distributions.** If your company's plan paid out any distributions during the year, report the amount to the IRS and the recipient on IRS Form 1099-R, Distributions from Pensions, Annuities, Retirement or Profit-Sharing Plans, IRAs, Insurance Contracts, Etc.

- **Retirement and employee benefit plans.** If you have a qualified retirement plan, such as a profit-sharing plan, you must report plan assets, liabilities, and annual contributions to the Employee Benefits Security Administration (not to the IRS) on an IRS form in the 5500 series (the type of return depends on the type of plan). However, no reporting is required for plans with assets under $100,000 for all years after 1993, as well as for simplified employee pensions (SEPs) and savings incentive match plan for employees individual retirement accounts (SIMPLE IRAs) regardless of assets.

- **Small cash transactions.** If your business sells or redeems money orders or traveler's checks in excess of $1,000 per customer per day or issues your own value cards, you are asked to report any suspicious transactions that exceed $2,000 to the U.S. Treasury. Such businesses are called money services businesses and include convenience stores, groceries, liquor stores, travel agencies, courier services and gas stations, all of which can be small businesses. This reporting is not mandatory; it is designed to identify individuals who provide false or expired identification or act suspicious. Reporting is made within 30 days of the suspicious activity on Treasury Department Form TD 90-22.56, Suspicious Activity Report by Money Services Businesses.

- *Wages.* See W-2 reporting listed under "Employment Taxes."

Property Taxes

If your business owns property or is required to pay for property taxes under a rental agreement (usually called a net lease), then this becomes another tax obligation to meet.

Property taxes for businesses can also extend to taxes on inventory and other personal property (personal in this case means not real estate; it doesn't mean you hold it for your own pleasure).

Strategies for Meeting Your Property Tax Obligations

Check for exemption to determine whether you have an obligation to pay property taxes in the first place. Some locations, for example, may exempt small businesses from filing a statement or return for personal property taxes. For instance, Los Angeles exempts businesses with personal property and fixtures costing less than $100,000 from submitting a property taxes return. The tax on these exempt businesses is the same from year to year unless adjusted by an on-site appraisal by a city tax assessor.

Reduce property taxes on inventory by selling or donating slow-moving inventory. Keeping items on your shelves that don't move can be costly not only in continued income tax, but also in personal property tax.

Check for tax reductions. Some states and localities that are aggressively trying to attract and retain businesses are now cutting property taxes. Don't assume that the amount you paid last year will be the same this year.

Sales and Use Taxes

The federal government does not have a sales or use tax. But states, counties, cities, and towns may impose their own sales tax. In fact, there are more than 7,500 different jurisdictions in the United States with a sales tax. There are also a corresponding number of places with a use tax, which is a tax imposed on the purchaser of goods from out-of-state vendors.

There is no denying that the rules for sales taxes are complex. Each jurisdiction has its own rules on which items are subject to the tax and which are exempt, and how to figure your tax obligations. For example, a jurisdiction may give you a choice between itemizing your sales taxes (reporting each tax collection for each taxable item sold) or applying an average rate based on your receipts.

Your Sales Tax Obligations

As a small-business owner you face two key obligations with respect to sales tax: collecting it from your customers and remitting it to the state agency in charge of collections.

Your obligation to collect sales tax usually applies only in a state in which you do business. So if you are a retail store in Florida and you sell an item to a customer in Arizona who asked that you ship it to her home, you do not have to be concerned with Arizona sales taxes. If the purchase is made in your store, you usually must collect sales tax, but there are exceptions when shipping out of state (check with your state taxing authority).

If you sell goods online, you may or may not have an obligation to collect sales tax on Internet sales. Clearly, customers in your state are subject to sales tax. But customers in other states may be exempt. First determine whether you have a presence in another state. For example, maintaining a server in another state *may* establish a nexus there. In one recent case, a California court concluded that Borders Online, a Delaware corporation that does not own or lease property in California or have any employees or a bank account in that state, nonetheless has a nexus there because online purchasers can return items to Borders stores in the state. Since the use of the Internet in commerce is relatively new, it is not well established in all jurisdictions whether sales to a customer in another state are subject to sales tax.

Caution: The Internet Tax Freedom Act banning sales tax on Internet access applies through November 1, 2007. This law does not affect sales taxes on goods and services sold online.

Getting a Resale Number

Your federal (or separate state) tax ID number is *not* the same as your state sales tax number (also referred to as a resale number, a seller's permit, or sales tax license). If you are just starting out in business, make sure to obtain your number. While it is necessary to have this number so you can collect sales tax on items you sell, it is also needed to avoid paying sales tax on items you buy for resale (i.e., inventory items).

Your resale number is obtained from your state. Some states assign a number that you can continue to use as long as you are in business; in other states the number must be renewed periodically. For details on obtaining your state resale number, contact your state tax, revenue, or finance department. Of course, states without sales tax (Alaska, Delaware, Montana, New Hampshire, and Oregon) do not issue resale numbers.

Your Use Tax Obligations

If you buy items in another state, you may owe use tax to your own state on the purchase. Your state, in effect, collects the amount of the sales tax you would have paid on the items if you have purchased them within your state. Usually, use tax is imposed on the purchaser, but some states collect it from the seller. This means you may have to self-assess the tax.

In deciding whether you owe use tax, check to see if there is an exemption for the item you have purchased. Exemptions may apply not only for items purchased for resale (e.g., inventory items), but also for items used for capital improvements or in research and development.

Excise Taxes

Prior to the advent of the federal income tax in 1913, excise taxes were the chief revenue source. Today, excise taxes continue to be imposed on the manufacture and distribution of certain nonessential consumer goods, such as spirits and tobacco, as well as on some services generally considered essential, such as telephone service and gasoline. Excise taxes include:

- Environment taxes on the sale or use of ozone-depleting chemicals.

- Communications and air transportation taxes.

- Fuel taxes.

- Manufacturer's taxes on various items (e.g., sportfishing equipment, bow-and-arrow components).

- Retailer tax on the sale of heavy trucks, trailers, and tractors (imposed on the seller).

There are no specific exemptions for small businesses, although only a limited number of small businesses may in fact be subject to these taxes. If you are liable for excise taxes, you must pay them to the government and file returns. You may be able to deduct excise taxes as a business expense.

LESSONS ABOUT TAXES

- ✔ Reporting income for tax purposes is both required by law and helpful for an owner's personal financial situation.

- ✔ Work with tax professionals to ease the burden of taxes on you and your business.

- ✔ Minimize income taxes to reduce the cost of doing business and retain more business profits.

- ✔ Plan ahead to meet your estimated tax obligations.

- ✔ Deposit payroll taxes on time to avoid penalties.

✔ File information returns when required to do so to avoid penalties.

✔ Obtain a sales tax number to avoid paying tax on items you buy for resale.

✔ Pay excise taxes if you manufacture or sell certain items.

Grow Your Business with Successful Marketing Strategies

Next to doing the right thing, the most important thing is to let people know you are doing the right thing.

—John D. Rockefeller

You can have the best product or service to offer, but if no one knows about it, you won't make any sales. The lifeblood of your business is marketing to create a continual stream of new customers to build your business and to maintain the flow of existing customers coming repeatedly back to you.

U.S. businesses would spend about $1.074 trillion in 2005 on marketing, according to projections in the Blackfriars Report "Marketing 2005: Sizing US Marketing" (June 2005). Small businesses account for only a tiny fraction of these dollars. It is challenging for small businesses to create effective marketing campaigns on limited budgets. Obviously, unlike major corporations, you can't afford to advertise on the Super Bowl or take full-page spreads in the New York Times or Sports Illustrated. But you can find ways to attract and retain customers to sell your products and services within your budget.

Marketing is a highly complex process, involving many different activities. As a first step in mastering the art of marketing, it is important to familiarize yourself with the different aspects of the process. Then you *can decide how much of these various activities to handle on your own and when to engage outside professionals to help you.*

In this chapter you will gain an understanding of the marketing process and learn to create your own effective marketing plan. You'll find out about how to promote yourself, often at no cost, and how to use advertising wisely. You'll learn about special marketing strategies for professionals, such as attorneys and accountants, who are barred from certain types of advertising. And you'll see how the Internet can be used in the marketing process.

Understand the Marketing Process

Marketing is often misunderstood; for example, some people confuse marketing with advertising. Marketing is an overall process in which customers get the goods and services they want and you get paid for what you sell so that you can make a profit. This rather simplistic definition, however, does not tell you all of the things involved in the process.

The marketing process really entails a number of steps, including:

- Market research to determine whether the public wants what you have to sell.

- Pricing to set the rate for your goods and services at a point that will allow you to generate maximum profit.

- Public relations to let the public know all about you.

- Advertising to inform the public of the features and benefits of the things you are selling.

- Distribution channels to get your products to customers (this isn't a concern if you're providing a service).

- Sales to convert interest in your products and services into dollars.

Be sure to attend to each of these steps and not to skip any one. Each step is explained in detail in this chapter. But first you need to develop a marketing plan that encompasses all of these steps.

Creating a Marketing Plan

To do any marketing, you need to know two things: how much you have to spend and how you are going to spend it. This means figuring a marketing budget and developing a marketing plan based on the money you have for this activity.

Figuring a Marketing Budget

How much should you spend on marketing? How much can you afford to spend? The right number depends on many factors, including the industry you are in, how aggressive you want to be in this activity, what your competition is doing, and what your revenue prospects are projected to be. Remember, like any other item in your budget, payment is supported by ongoing sales, not by past sales.

It has been widely accepted that large U.S. corporations spend about 6 percent of their gross revenues on marketing. Many small businesses, however, spend only leftover money—funds that are not allocated to rent or other expenses. A better strategy is to build a marketing number into your budget. As a rule of thumb, figure to spend between 4 and 10 percent of your gross revenues on your marketing activities. So if your gross revenues are $100,000 for 2006, expect to spend between $4,000 and $10,000 throughout the year on marketing activities.

Once you have a number, then refine your plan to allocate your annual expenditure among different marketing activities. Components of your marketing plan (many of which are discussed later in this chapter) may include some of the following activities:

- Advertising in print and media, including placement in the yellow pages.

- Branding activities.

- Direct marketing, including copywriting, printing, and postage.

- Entertainment and gifts for prospective and current customers.

- Events, such as seminars, networking, and in-house customer appreciation parties.

- Market research.

- Product packaging, including design and implementation.

- Public relations, which is the cost of hiring an outside PR agency.

- Sales activities (e.g., promotional coupons).

- Web site for development and maintenance, including pay-per-click search engine placements.

How much, if anything, you allocate to these activities depends a great deal on your type of business. Tradespeople and restaurants usually commit the bulk of their marketing dollars to yellow pages advertising. Professionals often put money into hosting events, entertainment, and, perhaps, PR activities. Manufacturers spend money on product packaging. Start-ups usually spend more in branding activities than established businesses do.

According to projections in the survey mentioned earlier (Blackfriars Report), in 2005 large corporations on average would allocate their marketing dollars as follows: 31 percent to advertising, 17 percent to web site development, 15 percent to events, and 10 percent to PR. Small companies may not want to follow this model, tailoring their budgets to more closely match their needs.

Small businesses that have a sound Web presence, for example, may want to spend as much as 25 percent of their total marketing budget on Web activities, including search engine placement. You may want to determine this allocation based on the anticipated return on investment—how much you expect to make on the money you spend. For instance, if you anticipate that your search engine placement efforts will result in 10,000 hits to your site, of which 100 will become customers (a 1 percent conversion rate) and you know that your average profit from each Web-based sale is $75, your breakeven point on search engine placement costs is $7,500 (10,000 hits times 1 percent conversion rate times $75 profit per sale). If you spend $3,600 on search engine placement for the year ($300 per month), you will have more than doubled your investment.

Developing a Marketing Plan

Since each company is unique, you need to craft a marketing plan that will serve your business needs. The plan includes your budget as well as your goals and the ways in which you expect to attain them.

To get you started in developing your own marketing plan,

you can find sample marketing plans (many of which are free) for various types of businesses, from accounting firms to bed-and-breakfasts to video stores, from Bplans.com at www.bplans .com/sp/marketingplans.cfm. You can take a free online tutorial on how to write a marketing plan from KnowThis.com at www.knowthis.com/general/marketplan.htm. You can purchase software to create your own marketing plan. Cost: about $100.

Reviewing Your Progress

Merely creating a marketing budget can be an ineffective step if you don't track your progress. Try to determine the effectiveness of your marketing program. The best measure (which is not always possible to determine) is your return on investment (ROI)—how much revenue you generated as a result of your marketing efforts. If you do a direct-mail campaign, you can divide the revenue from sales generated as a result of this effort by the cost of the campaign to determine your ROI. If a direct-mail campaign costs $2,500 and profits as a result are $5,000, your ROI is 200 percent.

Other measures include the number of sales leads generated and customer satisfaction. For instance, if you are a professional who gives a seminar that draws 25 prospects and you secure five people who want to personally discuss your services following the seminar, then determine what each of these hot leads cost you, based on your expenses in producing the seminar (e.g., advertising the seminar, renting a room, etc.).

Tracking advertising efforts can be difficult, but there are some effective strategies to use. For example, the owner of a temp agency in New York City tracked the effectiveness of her advertising by using a fictitious name in the ads. When prospects called in asking for that name, she knew the ad was responsible for the call. This same approach can be used for yellow pages advertising.

Market Research

Before you decide to sell something, it's a good idea to see if there is any need for or interest in your product or service. This determination is made through market research. Unfortunately,

many small businesses skip this step in the marketing process—
they think they're too small to conduct research or simply
ignore the need for this activity. Why should you do it? Here
are some determinations you must make and the reasons for doing so:

- *The size of your potential market*—anyone who might have an interest in buying what you sell and can afford it. For instance, are
  there a million people who might have an interest or only 100? If
  you find that the market is too small, it may not be worth the effort to go deeper into the marketing process.

- *Whom you are selling to*—by age, sex, location, education, house-
  hold income, and any other factors you deem relevant. This information is vital for you to do effective advertising.

- *The geographic boundaries*—whether your market is local (your
  neighborhood or city), regional (your county), national, or
  even international. With the Internet, even small businesses
  can compete on a grand scale never before possible. Again,
  determining your geographic boundaries helps you hone
  your advertising.

- *The competition.* It is very unusual for you to be the only business
  offering a particular product or service. It's more common that
  one or more competitors are already selling what you want to
  offer. Are you competing with high-end businesses or bargain
  basements? Are there many competitors or only a few? Knowing all about the competition can help you fix your prices so that
  you can find a niche in your market.

How to Do Market Research

You can do it yourself or use a company specializing in market research. The choice depends on your budget and how sophisticated
you want or need to be. Since market research means gathering information pertinent to your business, you can do this yourself in
an informal way. Here are some ideas to help you:

- Check the demographics of your market through information
  available at your local library or on the Internet.

- Conduct your own surveys and questionnaires.

- Test the waters. Try a sample ad to see if you draw any interest. Lillian Vernon, the mail order marketing pioneer, started her company with a single ad in *Seventeen* magazine. When she got an overwhelming response, she knew she was in business!

Pricing

What you charge for your goods or services is perhaps the single most important business decision you make. It means walking a fine line between charging enough to cover your expenses and make a profit, but not charging so much that customers buy elsewhere.

The price you set must be high enough to cover both expenses, including an income (salary) for you, and profit. You aren't a non-profit organization that can afford to merely cover costs, and this isn't a hobby run only for your own enjoyment. You need to set prices that will give you a reasonable return.

Only you know what your costs are and what you want or expect to earn from your business. In determining your costs, don't overlook *any* item you pay for, including taxes, travel expenses, and the elusive miscellaneous costs you haven't yet identified but know you'll incur.

How much profit should you build into the prices you charge? There is no single percentage or amount. It varies considerably from industry to industry, some working with lower profit margins than others. As a rule of thumb (especially for service-based businesses), you should aim for a 20 percent profit.

The business environment is constantly changing (for example, insurance costs for many types of coverage are continually escalating; competitors are entering or leaving the marketplace) and you must make sure your prices keep pace with these changes.

Make sure to check your pricing on a regular basis, no less frequently than once a year. Before raising prices, try cutting costs so that your profit from each sale can be maintained.

Pricing for Service-Based Businesses

There are four main ways to charge for your work:

1. *An hourly rate*—generally used when a job is labor intensive or when the nature of the job is expected to keep changing. This may be the best way to cover yourself when you can't be sure how much of your time a job will require.

2. *Unit pricing*—used when work is repetitive and the nature of the work is well known. For example, if your business is printing and related services, you can use unit pricing for photocopying jobs; you know at the start what it costs you to make each copy and can fix this in a unit price.

3. *By the job*—generally used for large projects involving costs you are certain of.

4. *Contingency*—based on performance. For example, an attorney may charge one-third of any money recovered for you.

In order to evaluate potential jobs, it is advisable to use estimating software that lets you fix a cost for each task involved in a project so you can simply figure the hourly or unit rate for each aspect.

You can combine pricing methods for a particular project. For example, you can set a price for a project, detailing exactly what the price covers, and include an hourly rate for any extras that arise.

How much should you be charging per hour? Obviously, it varies considerably with the type of service you provide. Professionals, such as accountants and architects, can charge more than gardeners and interior decorators, even though all provide services in a professional manner.

The basic formula for all types of service businesses is simply earnings (overhead expenses and your salary plus a profit) divided by billable hours. If you assume a 40-hour week, then billable hours for the year are 2,080 (40 hours × 52 weeks). However, many industries, such as Web designers, assume that there is a certain percentage of downtime—as much as 20 percent to 40 percent—and reduce their assumed billable hours accordingly. For the sake of simplicity, using a 1,600-hour year as a pricing basis may be more realistic for some industries.

For example, if you believe your skills should merit $60,000 per year, your overhead is $40,000, and you want a 20 percent profit (figured as a percentage of your earnings plus overhead), you'll have to bill $75 per hour [($60,000 + $40,000 + $20,000) ÷ 1,600].

Obviously, you can't fix your prices in a vacuum. Your final price must reflect the pressures from your competition (something you've determined in your market research). Location may also play a role in setting your prices. Don't set your prices so high that you price yourself out of the market or so low that you fail to make a profit. If pricing puts you at the high end of the market, make sure you can justify it to your customers—by quality, uniqueness, and the like.

Be sure to know your margins. They will determine the degree of flexibility you have if you have to offer a lower price for a special customer.

You can also adjust your prices for any value-added services that you can provide for which the customer is willing to pay, such as a guaranteed performance date, same-day shipping, and so on.

Pricing for Product-Based Businesses

If you sell specific items, you have to fix a unit price for each item. The same basic concepts used in figuring an hourly rate apply to this type of pricing; you simply include your cost of goods sold (what it cost you to buy or build the item) as part of your overhead.

However, it may be better to figure your break-even point on each item by not building in a profit margin—you can then tack on a profit figure per unit. The break-even point generally varies with the quantity sold since fixed expenses are spread among a greater number of units, called economy of scale. In fixing your price, don't ignore depreciation of equipment, a noncost expense you should take into account as part of your overhead.

If you cut the price of a unit, will it drive up sales, enabling you to boost overall profits? Before you answer, keep in mind that your intentions may not translate into sales if competitors also slash prices.

Depending upon the industry, the practice of discounting—

giving customers a price reduction, usually as a percentage of the price—is a common practice. In figuring your unit pricing, you need to build in a sufficient cushion to allow for routine discounting.

Special Rules for Online Pricing

Customers who buy online commonly expect to see bargains—prices that are discounted from those in stores. According to Ernst & Young, the average discount offered online by retailers who also maintain bricks-and-mortar stores is 10 percent. Certain types of products, such as books, command a higher online discount.

Public Relations

Whether you do it yourself or use a public relations agency, you need to continually promote your business and yourself. It's all about your message—what you want to convey to the public about you and your business. PR typically isn't about your product or service; it's usually all about you. The goal of PR is to create a favorable opinion about you and your company in the minds of a target audience—potential customers, media, and the like.

Today, PR often involves creating a brand or identity for your business. You are undoubtedly familiar with brand enhancers such as the Nike swoosh, IBM's nickname Big Blue, and McDonald's restaurants' golden arches. These brands have become synonymous with the products that these companies sell. Branding is more than a logo—it encompasses an image, concept, and reputation linked inextricably to your business, with the goal of establishing credibility for the products and services you sell. So PR may entail redesigns of your company logo, stationery, signs, and every other public representation of your business.

PR usually involves a wide range of other activities designed to bring you into the public's eye. These include:

- *Press releases.* These tell the public something new or special about you: a new product you are about to introduce, a new office you have just opened, a company anniversary (e.g., five years in business), or any other newsy thing about you or your business.

- *Publicity events.* Also called publicity stunts, these are intended to attract media attention. They can include grand openings and other events that are not staged.

- *Media appearances.* Radio and TV appearances allow you to gain wide exposure for yourself and your company. Usually, the opportunity for these appearances is limited to unusual events, such as a dramatically good or bad happening.

- *Writings.* Newspaper columns, articles, and books give you an opportunity for a byline, which is a mention of your name, company, and, often, contact information (e.g., web site or location).

- *Talks.* Speaking before community organizations, professional groups, or associations helps you feature your expertise and provides exposure for you and your company.

Teaming Up with Other Businesses and Organizations

You can enhance your image by establishing relationships with better-known entities. For example, a company that services small businesses might want to ally itself with the Small Business Administration. In this case, you gain respectability and reliability through association.

Self-Promotion

Sure, we hate to brag. Our parents told us that it's not polite to do so. But when it comes to our businesses, bragging is a necessary part of marketing. You have to share the good points about you and your company in order to generate sales.

Self-promotion for small businesses doesn't have to be costly. There are many ways in which to keep your name before the public for little or no money. Here are some strategies to explore:

- *Charity events.* If you are involved with local charities, there may be opportunities for your business to do some self-promotion.

Personally become active in an organization, so that you not only help your favorite cause but also gain exposure for your company. An insurance agent on the board of the local American Cancer Society worked on its major fund-raising activities. During the course of these activities, he met and befriended many local business owners, a number of whom subsequently became his clients.

- *Sponsorship of local sports teams.* If you are involved in local sports, such as Little League, consider adding your company name to a team. Sponsorship is not pricey, but can engender a lot of local goodwill.

- *Word of mouth.* The best form of advertising is also the cheapest: getting your existing customers to tell others about you. Referrals for some types of businesses, such as law firms, are usually the prime way in which to obtain new business. *Always* ask existing customers for referrals; not all will respond, but many do. Thank customers for referrals with a kind word or some money-saving offer (e.g., a free item when a new customer signs on).

Advertising

Most businesses must advertise, to a greater or lesser extent, in order to attract customers. John Wanamaker, the famous U.S. department store merchant, said, "Half the money I spend on advertising is wasted; the trouble is I don't know which half." Unless referrals or other connections can direct a steady stream of business to your door, be prepared to spend money on advertising.

Advertising can take many forms, but all of these forms fall into two broad categories: direct and indirect advertising. Direct advertising is, as the name implies, in-your-face promotion about what you are selling. For example: "Beautiful hand-knit sweaters" or "Quality Web design services."

Indirect advertising is a little more subtle, involving promotion of your company as well as the items or services you sell.

This type of advertising involves the use of a company logo to develop awareness of your business. As the public grows to recognize your logo, it will embrace what you have to sell because of your name as much as the features of the things you are selling.

Advertising can be costly, but you can advertise without blowing your entire marketing budget on a single effort. Keep in mind that the key to successful advertising is repetition, although it's impossible to say how much repetition is needed. It's safe to say that just one ad in a magazine may prove totally ineffective in attracting new customers. It's probably a good idea to pick one method of advertising and stick with it for a while. Don't start one month and stop the next.

Decide whether to handle your own advertising or use an agency or other professionals to assist you. Obviously there is a cost factor to consider. Agencies charge for their services, but may be able to negotiate better placements and cheaper rates than you can.

Some of the most common ways for small businesses to advertise include:

- *Telephone directories.* If your business is primarily local, then advertising in the yellow pages of your telephone directory may be advisable. Some of the most popular ads include those for trades (e.g., electricians and plumbers); restaurants; and professionals (e.g., doctors, dentists, and attorneys). The reason: Consumers are attuned to looking for these businesses in the telephone book. Choose the directory that is best for you: The primary directory is the Yellow Pages published by the regional Baby Bells. However, there are numerous other directories, including Yellow Book (published in 42 states) and various local directories (e.g., local directories for Spanish-speaking businesses). Having a business telephone number automatically entitles you to a free listing in all yellow pages directories. But to stand out from your competitors, you need to pay for larger ads. The amount you pay depends on the market you are in (New York City costs more than most suburban areas) and on the size of the ad you take (a full-page ad can be pricey, but a quarter-column ad may be well within your budget). Also obtain a listing for your web site in Internet yellow pages.

- *Online directories.* Consumers are increasingly turning to the Web for all their buying needs. If you sell products beyond your locality, you may want to spend some advertising dollars for listings in Google, Yahoo!, and other search engines. The cost of advertising here is a charge for each visitor you obtain through the search engine ("pay per click"). You may pay as little as a penny or two to draw a visitor to your site, but usually the cost is higher.

- *Local newspapers and* **Pennysavers.** This form of print advertising can be useful for certain types of businesses. For example, tradespeople and restaurants frequently use local *Pennysavers*, distributed weekly to all households in the area, as a low-cost advertising medium.

- *Community mailers.* Send out coupons to local households and businesses as inducements to buy your goods or services. Val-pak (www.valpak.com and click on "advertising information"), which reaches nearly 50 million households and businesses nationwide, is another inexpensive way to advertise.

Make sure your advertising complies with all law requirements. For example, you cannot use false or deceptive ads and you must have proof to back up any claims you make. To learn the rules, view "A Guide for Small Business: General Advertising Policies" from the Federal Trade Commission at www.ftc.gov (click on "For Business," then "Advertising Guidance," then "Frequently Asked Advertising Questions").

Distribution

How do the items you sell get into the hands of customers? The items must go through (distribution) channels. These include retail, wholesale, mail order, Internet, direct sales, or selling through sales agents. Understand each of these options so you can decide which venue is best suited for what you sell.

Say you are selling vitamins and other health products. What distribution method is best for you? Consider your alternatives: To sell retail would mean opening up a store that competes with Walgreens, General Nutrition Centers (GNC), and other national retailers that also sell vitamins. Wholesaling your vitamins would mean convincing these national retailers to stock your items on their shelves. Mail order requires you to find potential customers that you can send catalogs to; Internet means posting your vitamins on a web site—yours or some site for online stores. Direct sales are face-to-face selling outside of a store, a catalog, or the Internet—the type of sales that Avon and Mary Kay do for cosmetics. Selling through sales agents probably would mean they, rather than you, do direct sales on your behalf.

Once you review your alternatives, then select the best means for your items. Factors in making your decision include cost (obviously a retail store is a more costly alternative to direct sales); the nature of what you sell (services versus products, and which products); and the size of your budget (if you start on a shoestring, you may not be able to afford a pricey location in an affluent suburban mall). Depending on the things you sell, you can combine two or more venues. For instance, a custom-furniture maker might sell retail as well as online through his own web site.

Fulfillment

If you sell high-volume items and want to grow your business, you may be unable to handle things on your own. You can add to your staff. But you might consider using an outside company dedicated to filling your orders. Called a fulfillment company, this type of business can take orders, store products, and ship them—for a fee.

Sales

Converting a customer's wants or needs into an immediate desire for the things you sell is what selling is all about. Selling is clearly a skill, and not everyone can master it. But small business owners often find themselves as the chief (or only) salesperson in their company. Here are five steps to nailing down a sale:

- *Step 1: Identify the prospect's needs.* Unless there is an immediate, and often pressing, need on the part of a prospect that you can fill or solve, it's unlikely you'll get a sale. It can take prodding and persistence to uncover the needs before you can demonstrate why you are the customer's answer to his or her problem. Where appropriate, take the time to connect to the person so he or she will open up to you, enabling you to learn the real needs.

- *Step 2: Make an offer.* Depending on what you sell, it may be a straightforward offer or entail a lengthy and detailed written description of the goods and services you can provide. For instance, a customer searching for a new winter coat has a clear need; you can make a proposal by suggesting she purchase this coat or that. But if a customer is looking for Web design or architectural plans for a new home, you may be required to sketch out or provide in-depth plans for consideration.

- *Step 3: Address the prospect's objections.* These may be about your prices, your promised delivery time, or other parts of the transaction. Try to find out what's holding up a response. Prospects can respond to you in one of three ways: yes, no, or I'll have to think it over. If you can't obtain an immediate yes, it's probably better to try for a firm no if there is really no interest, so you don't continue to waste your, and the customer's, time.

- *Step 4: Negotiate terms, where applicable.* If you charge a fixed rate, you may have very little ability to maneuver—a $100 pair of shoes or $75 for a teeth cleaning may be your going rate, offered on a take-it-or-leave-it basis. But often you can find some way to compromise, if not on price then on other terms, such as the time of delivery or performance.

- *Step 5: Close the sale.* A sale is not final until you are paid. Tie down a prospect by getting an immediate purchase or a firm commitment. If you've completed steps 1 through 4 successfully, step 5 should be no problem. If you fail to get the prospect to sign on the dotted line, then you've probably failed at one of the previous steps. You may be able to go back and correct a defect, or decide that the only thing to do at this point is move on to a new prospect.

Promotion

To stimulate action on the part of customers, consider using promotional methods. These include:

- Discount coupons.

- Special pricing—buy one, get one free.

- Bonuses—a free item with a certain level of sales.

- Buyer clubs—to build up credits for future purchases.

Professionals may want to offer some free time, such as a one-hour consultation, to attract new business. Just recognize that some tire kickers will use up the time but won't pay for additional help.

Special Marketing Strategies for Professionals

Ethics for various professionals limit the types of marketing that can be done. For instance, attorneys cannot offer financial inducements to existing clients for referrals. And, because of the rules on confidentiality, they cannot publicize their client list. Learn the limitations, if any, of your profession before crafting a marketing strategy.

Professionals often do best in marketing through networking, hosting seminars, and obtaining referrals from existing clients. For example, a financial planner in Fort Lauderdale gives free seminars on estate planning as a way to attract new clients. But these traditional marketing venues are not your only options. Other ways to market your professional skills is through an informational web site (see next section) and by partnering informally with other professionals who do not compete with you. For instance, an accountant specializing in small businesses may partner informally with an attorney who also handles small businesses as a way for each one to obtain more clients.

Using the Internet for Marketing

There are a number of ways in which you can use the Internet for marketing. You can maintain a web site to highlight your company features, advertise on search engines, and, in some cases, sell your products or services.

Web Site

Today just about every small business needs an Internet presence. It is a sign of an established business. And, of course, it is a way to attract new customers and grow your business. Decide what function your web site will serve to your business—branding, online store—so that you can tailor your site accordingly.

Creating and maintaining a web site can entail a considerable financial investment. You have to pay for:

- *Domain name.* This is a fee for a year, two years, five years, or more that protects your web site *address*, called your URL (universal resource locator). Cost: usually $35 for one year; under $300 for 10 years. As a small business, your URL extension—the three letters after the dot—is usually "com." However, you can use "biz" or, if your company is involved in the Internet, "net."

- *Web design.* Here's where your budget dictates your design. If you want a Web designer to create a unique Internet presence for your company, expect to spend about $10,000 or more. However, you can get your own web site customized for your business if you do it yourself for as little as a few dollars a month. In between is a great variety of Web design assistance, using template-based designs.

- *Hosting and storage.* You need a Web host company that can store your site for you. This is a monthly cost, the amount of which can depend on the size of your site. The more pages and pictures you have (the larger your storage needs), the greater your monthly fee.

- *Site maintenance.* You can set up your site so that you have the ability to continually update your information by yourself, without the need for a programmer or Web designer. However, if you are not up to this task, then you'll incur ongoing site maintenance costs.

Attracting visitors to your site is only half the battle. Once you have captured their attention, you want to accomplish several objectives:

- *Reinforce your brand.* Your site should reflect your company identity (discussed earlier in this chapter). Make sure you include your logo and have your site leave visitors with the impression you want to convey.

- *Gather information.* You want to know who visits your site so that you can approach them later for sales. You can collect this data by asking visitors to register at your site. Usually, you must offer something of value in return, such as a free newsletter or a free consultation.

- *Give to get.* In order to attract visitors to your site, you must offer something of interest *besides* what you have to sell. This can be links to other sites, general information about a subject, or news that visitors will be thankful for.

- *Repeat visitors.* Your site must contain something that visitors want to return to over and over again. This is called a "sticky" site because visitors stick with you, returning to view your new material on a regular basis. Garnering repeat visitors requires you to change information, offers, or other features on the site, such as a "tip of the day" that changes every 24 hours.

- *Contact information.* Your site must enable visitors to get in touch with you. It's usually best to offer a number of alternatives on ways to contact you, including a telephone number, e-mail address, and snail-mail address.

Advertising on Other Web Sites

You can use the Internet as an advertising medium, usually as a draw to your own web site. Instead of placing ads in print or radio and TV, consider ads on the Internet.

Banner ads are visual graphics displayed on web sites other than yours. You may pay on a weekly or some other basis. The cost depends on where your ad runs—the better known the site, the more you'll pay. Size and frequency of your ad also affect price.

Blogging

The term "blog," a contraction of "Web log," first coined in 1999, became mainstream in 2005 when it entered the Merriam-Webster dictionary. A blog is a collection of self-published pieces of information stored on the Internet for access by the Web community. Blogs were started in 1997 by techies providing technology-related information to one another in an open format. According to Technorati, the authority in the world of blogs (www.technorati.com), in December 2005 there were an estimated 23.1 billion blogs, and the number is increasing as blogs are being used by businesses as a marketing tool to introduce the business and its products to the public. Unlike typical Web pages that are read-only, a blog lets the reader respond and become part of the blog for the public to see. Here's how you can use blogging in your marketing efforts:

- *Inform consumers of a new product or idea.* Use blogging to spread the word. Readers will gobble up information, which hopefully you can then turn into sales.

- *Obtain customer feedback.* Use blogging to improve your products or services by soliciting customer ideas.

- *Become an industry expert.* Use blogging to enhance your credibility as an expert on a particular subject. This creates positive buzz in your field.

- *Obtain an Internet presence at a fraction of the cost of a web site.* You don't need to pay a webmaster or learn hypertext markup language (HTML) to gain a foothold on the Web.

- *Leverage your search engine ranking.* Use blogging to ratchet up the number of hits on your site, which improves your listings in Google, Yahoo!, MSN, and other search engines. Every new posting by a viewer is treated as another web page containing keywords that will be noticed by search engines.

To be effective, keep your blog short and entertaining. Typically blogs are written informally in the first person. They are usually only a paragraph or two in length. Include links to your company site. But before making a commitment to blog, be sure you are up to the task. You should be prepared to update your blog regularly (some are updated daily; others several times a day!).

To see how small businesses are using blogs and get helpful information for your business blogging, go to:

- Blog Business World (www.blogbusinessworld.blogspot.com), containing blogs in business, marketing, public relations, and search engine optimization for successful entrepreneurs. The site also offers links to blog resources.

- Small Biz Advisor (www.small-biz-advisor.com/news/blog/default.aspx), providing information on how to maintain the image of a big company without spending a lot of money. It is an offshoot of Neodex Press, a small publishing company in Seattle, Washington.

- Business Blogging Bootcamp (http://windsormedia.blogs.com/businessbloggingbootcamp), a place to receive basic training in what the site calls WMC (weapon of mass communication). The blog is provided by marketing expert Yvonne DiVita of Windsor Media Enterprises, LLC.

- The Small Business Blog (www.sbblog.com).

- Dane Carlson's Business Opportunities Weblog (www.business-opportunities.biz), a moderated list of business opportunities presented in chronological order.

- What's Your Brand Mantra? (http://brand.blogs.com/mantra), containing musings on branding by Jennifer Rice, whose company Mantra Brand Communications does brand strategy consulting.

Blogging tools are available at Movable Type (www.sixapart.com/movabletype), Blogger.com (www.blogger.com/start),

MyBlogSite (www.myblogsite.com/?sid=GOOGLEblog), and Radio Userland (http://radio.userland.com).

E-mail

Sending notices, advertisements, and announcements via e-mail is a low-cost way to reach a large number of people. You can send to your existing customers, to e-mail addresses you gather at your site, or to e-mail lists that you can rent. The downside is that an increasing number of people have security measures on their systems to block certain types of e-mail that may include what you are sending, so your message won't get through. Still, e-mail can be an effective marketing tool.

In using e-mail, be sure to avoid illegal spamming. The Controlling the Assault of Non-Solicited Pornography and Marketing (CAN-SPAM) Act of 2003, which became effective in 2004, establishes rules for the use of commercial e-mail. If you violate these rules, you can be subject to penalties and, even worse, have your Internet access blocked.

Under this law, your routing information must be accurate. This is easily accomplished when you send e-mails from your company address. Your subject line cannot be false or misleading. If you are sending an advertisement, you must identify the e-mail as such and include your postal address. You must also give recipients a way to opt out of receiving further e-mails from you. Your opt-out mechanism must be processed within 30 days.

LESSONS ABOUT MARKETING

✔ Understand the marketing process.

✔ Develop a marketing budget.

✔ Create a marketing plan.

✔ Do market research to determine the level of interest for your products or services.

✔ Set your prices to maximize your sales.

✔ Use public relations to spread your message.

✔ Advertise on a regular and consistent basis.

✔ Determine the best means of distribution for your products.

✔ Follow the steps through the sales process to close the deal.

✔ Use the Internet wisely for your marketing efforts.

PART THREE

THE UNEXPECTED SIDE OF BUSINESS

Use Legal Protections

I don't know as I want a lawyer to tell me what to do. I hire him to tell me how to do what I want to do.

—J. P. Morgan, financier

ost people in business who have had to deal with the legal system would agree with Shakespeare to kill all the lawyers. Attorneys can be very expensive and often won't give you the black-and-white answers you want or need to run your business. But you can't escape the need to use legal protections in order to operate your business if you want to sleep at night and stay out of trouble. And to do this effectively, you usually have to turn to attorneys for guidance.

Lawyers can help you at all stages of your business, from start-up through growth and during your exit phase. Hopefully, the advice you follow will keep problems from arising. But if problems do arise, again you may need the assistance of attorneys to help you through troubled times.

You can gain some legal protection through your own efforts; sometimes, however, you need professional assistance. To the extent you can clearly identify your legal issues and understand your alternatives, you can reduce the time it will take for a professional to produce for you, reducing the cost of legal assistance.

This chapter explains how to set up your business in such a way as to obtain legal protection for yourself. It also shows how to protect your business property. You'll see how to use contracts and agreements in dealing with customers, suppliers, and other parties. You'll find out how to research some legal questions on your own. And, finally, you'll learn how a buy-sell agreement can protect you and your co-owners when death or other events transpire.

Business Structure

The way in which you set up your company can affect your personal exposure for business debts. For instance, if a customer is injured on your premises and insurance doesn't cover damages, are you personally liable for these damages? The answer depends on how you've structured your business from a legal standpoint.

In some types of businesses, owners remain personally liable for business debts. This means that creditors may be able to take your home, your personal bank account, and other assets to pay off business debts. In other types of businesses, creditors can look only to business assets to satisfy their claims; you are not personally liable for business debt.

The following types of business structures provide personal liability protection. Each of these structures can be used whether you are the only owner or you have one or more co-owners.

- *Limited liability companies (LLCs).* These are companies set up under state law that allow owners (called members) to gain personal liability protection without forgoing the tax advantages of partnerships.

- *S corporations.* These are corporations set up under state law that elect to be taxed as pass-through entities; the shareholders and not the corporation usually are the taxpayers on business profits. Shareholders are not personally liable for corporate debts.

- *C corporations.* These are corporations (sometimes referred to as regular corporations) set up under state law that operate as separate taxpaying entities. Shareholders are not personally liable for corporate debts.

Sole proprietorships, independent contractors, and partnerships do not provide personal liability protection. However, limited partnerships, a type of partnership set up under state law, offer personal liability protection for limited partners; general partners remain personally liable for business debts.

Choosing Your Structure

The type of business you form is a multifaceted decision. It involves not only your desire for legal protection but also tax and other considerations. Your decision also depends in part on the number and nature of the owners, the type of industry you are in, and your personal inclinations. In addition to personal liability discussed earlier, consider the following factors in making your decision.

COST

There is virtually no cost to forming a sole proprietorship. You may have to file a form with your city or county to say you are doing business under a name that is different from your own, such as the Sunshine Flower Shop (called filing a "DBA" or "doing business as" form), but the fee is usually modest (e.g., $35) and you don't need a lawyer to handle this for you. Partnerships are similarly inexpensive to form, although it is highly advisable to have a partnership agreement spelling out the terms and conditions among partners—and you should have an attorney draw this up for you or at least review your self-drafted or preprinted agreement.

When forming a corporation or an LLC, there are state filing fees and publication costs (for example, you may have to place a public notice in your local newspaper that you have formed an LLC). There are many do-it-yourself web sites for incorporation and LLC formation (e.g., BizFilings at www.bizfilings.com). However, you may want to use an attorney; this is a one-time cost and, for attorneys, a routine matter that is not highly billed.

PUBLIC PERCEPTION

The more favorably the public views your business, the more this translates into increased sales and other opportunities. Generally, organizing as an LLC or a corporation so that you can display "LLC" or "Inc.," "Corp.," or "Ltd." after your business name may raise public confidence in your business. It's usually believed that these business entities are more permanent than sole proprietorships and partnerships. Banks may also prefer to give loans to corporations and LLCs over sole proprietorships and partnerships.

TAXES

To retain more of your profits, you naturally want to cut taxes (legally of course). Your form of entity can impact your bottom line.

Owners of all types of entities other than a C corporation pay taxes on their share of business profits on their personal returns. Only C corporations pay tax on their own returns. There are separate graduated rates for individuals and C corporations—the top rate for both is 35 percent. But C corporations pay ordinary tax rates on capital gains; individuals pay no more than 15 percent on long-term capital gains. For losses, individual owners claim them on their personal returns *unless* the business is a C corporation; only the corporation can deduct its losses.

State tax rules are another consideration—the treatment for federal taxes may not be followed in the states (e.g., some states do not recognize S corporations and tax them as regular corporations).

There are some restrictions on the use of accounting periods and accounting methods for certain entities. For example, partnerships and S corporations usually must use a calendar year (rather than a fiscal year) to report income. C corporations usually must use the accrual method of accounting (rather than the cash method).

And your risk of facing an IRS audit varies with your business form. Partnerships have exceedingly low audit rates; sole proprietorships have comparatively high audit rates.

Finally, think about the taxes imposed when a business terminates. Having a C corporation, for example, may result in double taxation: once at the corporate level and again at the owner level.

FRINGE BENEFITS

The tax law is peppered with a number of tax-free fringe benefits. However, in many cases benefits are not tax free to owners. Owners whose businesses can afford to provide benefits may want to use a C corporation in order to take advantage of fringe-benefit opportunities.

NATURE AND NUMBER OF OWNERS

How many co-owners you have and whether they are individuals (U.S. or foreign) or other business entities affect your decision. For example, S corporations cannot have any shareholders who are nonresident aliens, partnerships, or corporations. And they are limited to 100 eligible shareholders (though this is usually not a problem for small businesses). Partnerships, by definition, must have two or more owners; sole proprietorships cannot have more than one owner.

SOCIAL SECURITY AND MEDICARE TAXES

Where owners work for their companies, the payment of Social Security and Medicare taxes becomes important. For an employee, the employer and employee each pay these taxes on compensation. In 2006, the tax is 7.65 percent on wages up to $94,200 and 1.45 percent on wages over $94,200. A self-employed individual pays both the employer and employee share on his or her share of company profits (15.3 percent on net earnings from self-employment up to $94,200 in 2006; 2.9 percent on net earnings over this limit). Owners who work for their corporations can minimize exposure to these taxes by taking only modest salaries. Owners who have a sole proprietorship, partnership, or limited liability company pay the full tax, regardless of their draw (although one-half of these taxes is deductible).

MULTISTATE OPERATIONS

Each state has its own tax rules for businesses. Don't assume that the way in which you organize your company for federal tax purposes will necessarily control for state tax purposes. As mentioned earlier, some states do not recognize S corporations; these corporations are not federal taxpayers but do pay state corporate income taxes. Since a business must file returns and pay taxes to each state in which it has a nexus (a business connection such as maintaining an office or a sales force), it usually makes sense to operate as a C corporation—only the corporation files returns in each state in which it does business. In contrast, if the business were an LLC with five co-owners, then each owner must file a return in each of these states. One such LLC did business in 19 states, so its owners

had to file personal returns in all of these states, for a total of 95 returns (5 owners times 19 states)!

What does all this mean? The decision on how to form your
business isn't a simple one and isn't limited to your desire for personal liability protection. If you are a freelance writer, the need for
personal liability protection is very minimal and operating as a
sole proprietor may make sense. But if you make a lot of money,
becoming an S corporation and taking a modest salary can cut
way down on employment taxes.

You probably should discuss your situation with a tax professional who can help you evaluate all of the factors. And, if you decide to incorporate, should you do so in your home state, or in
Delaware or Nevada? Usually your home state is the best place,
but if you operate in more than one state, Delaware or Nevada
may make sense—something an attorney could advise you on.

Changing Your Structure

Just because you've been operating as a sole proprietorship does
not mean you can't change your business structure. After considering all of the aforementioned factors, maybe you think you need
personal liability protection or would appear more businesslike if
you had an "Inc." or "LLC" after your company name.

You can change structures, but consider the costs. There are legal costs—filing and attorney's fees—for incorporating or forming
an LLC. There are also accounting costs to change your accounting
system.

And there may be tax costs. There is usually no tax cost to incorporate or form an LLC for your sole proprietorship. But if you
have a C corporation and want to switch to LLC status, you may
incur a tax when liquidating the corporation.

Protecting Intellectual Property

Some of the most valuable assets of any business are its intellectual property. Intellectual property (IP) is an intangible asset: You
can't touch it, see it, or smell it, but you know it's there and it can

be worth a lot of money to your business. IP includes such items as goodwill, customer lists, patents, copyrights, trademarks, trade names, and service marks.

You can protect some IP through your own internal procedures and efforts. For example, you can make sure that customer lists remain private by educating employees on the need to keep the lists private and by having them sign confidentiality agreements (discussed later in this chapter).

Some types of IP, however, require legal action to secure protection. For example, you protect an invention or process usually only by obtaining a patent from the U.S. Patent and Trademark Office (USPTO) (www.uspto.gov). You do not gain any protection merely by labeling a product "patent pending" or "patent applied for." It is unlawful to do this unless you have begun the patent process, and you may be subject to penalties for false labeling.

Patents

A patent gives you an exclusive right to use your idea for a product or process for a limited period of time. It is a property right granted by the federal government. Patent protection lasts for 17 years (14 years for design patents). During this period, you can use your idea exclusively or license it to others. After this period, it is part of the public domain and anyone can use it without permission from or payment to you.

Getting a patent can be a lengthy and costly legal process. First decide whether you want patent protection; you may be able to treat your idea as a trade secret and protect it accordingly. Coca-Cola never patented its soda flavor. Instead it has closely guarded the recipe as a trade secret for more than 100 years. If you want patent protection, decide how much you can do yourself to save money and when you need to call in an expert.

To obtain a patent, you must demonstrate to the U.S. Patent and Trademark Office that your idea is unique and has not been patented before. Follow these steps in the patent process:

1. *Document your idea.* Keep a notebook as you develop your idea, noting the date of each step.

2. *Establish your time line.* Write a description of your idea, sign it before a notary public, seal the signed statement in an envelope, and mail it to yourself using registered mail. Keep it in a safe place and do not open it unless and until you do so in a court proceeding to establish rights to a patent.

3. *Use a disclosure document from the U.S. Patent and Trademark Office.* File this form with the USPTO, along with photocopies or photographs of the idea or drawing and a $10 filing fee. The purpose of this document is to establish the date of conception—it does not give you any patent protection. But it can be helpful in raising money from investors because it shows you have begun the patent process.

4. *Obtain a patent.* Get an experienced patent attorney or patent agent on board to help you with this process. It can take some time, from preliminary searches to the final grant of the patent. It can also take a lot of money; expect to pay thousands of dollars (depending on what you are patenting) in expert assistance fees and hundreds of dollars in filing fees and other costs (although "small entities"—independent inventors and small businesses—pay half the normal fees).

Copyrights

You obtain a copyright for creative works, which include not only literary works, art, and music, but also fabrics, games, and computer software automatically when the work is created and is fixed in a copiable form (e.g., a cassette tape or CD for a musical work). The work does not have to be "published" (that is, offered for sale to the public). But simply affixing the copyright symbol to the work does not endow it with rights (such the right to file a lawsuit for infringement) that can be obtained only by formal registration.

Copyright protection gives you the exclusive right to market your work for the life of the author plus 70 years for works originally created on or after January 1, 1978. Works done "for hire" and anonymous and pseudonymous works have different protection periods.

Copyright registration is obtained by filing for it with the Register of Copyrights, Copyright Office, Library of Congress (www.copyright.gov). There is usually a registration fee of $30. Once you have registered your work, you can protect it by displaying the symbol ©. You can download required forms and filing procedures from this site if you want to handle registration by yourself.

Trademarks

A trademark is protection for a name, word, phrase, symbol, or design or a combination of words, phrases, symbols, or designs that identify or distinguish the source of goods and services. A service mark is the same as a trademark, except that it serves to distinguish a service rather than a product. For purposes of this discussion, the generic term *trademark*, commonly used to cover both categories, is explained.

There are three ways in which to obtain trademark protection:

1. *Common law.* A mark used for goods or services belongs to the one who created it. You can show the public that *you* created the words, symbol, or design by designating it with a ™ or ℠ symbol. The mark does not have to be registered, and you do not even have to apply for registration in order to use the mark. However, the mark does not establish your claim of creation.

2. *State trademark laws.* Under the laws in each state, trademarks are protected as part of the law of unfair competition, and registration is not required. However, for businesses operating across state lines, including those with Internet sales, state trademark protection may be inadequate to protect against infringement.

3. *Federal trademark law.* To gain nationwide protection for your words, symbol, or design, it's advisable to register with the U.S. Patent and Trademark Office. This allows you to display the symbol ®. Federal protection lasts for 10 years, with 10-year renewable periods. After the fifth year of registration, you must file an affidavit with certain information in order to keep the trademark alive and the option for renewals open. To obtain federal trademark protection, you must have a

trademark in use in interstate commerce. You can do this by affixing your mark to a product and shipping it to a customer in another state. The fee for registration is $325 if filed electronically or $375 if filed by paper.

Secrets and Ideas

If you have some trade secret, idea, or process that cannot be patented, copyrighted, or trademarked, you can still protect it. While there is no federal right of protection or registration, there may be state law protection. Guard a trade secret, idea, or process as you would any secret. Keep the idea in a safe place. Mark any correspondence or files in which you use the idea as "confidential" or "secret." And, as discussed earlier, teach your staff to guard your secrets and have them sign nondisclosure agreements.

If you do business overseas, don't assume that your domestic protection extends to violations in foreign countries. For foreign protection, you must follow different rules:

- *Patents.* Under the Patent Cooperation Treaty, you can submit one international patent application to obtain protection in 126 countries (go to www.uspto.gov/go/pct).

- *Trademarks.* Under the Madrid Protocol, applications in separate countries are made easier (for example, you can submit an application in English) (go to www.uspto.gov/web/trademarks/madrid/madridindex.htm).

For more information about worldwide protection, see the World Intellectual Property Organization (WIPO) at www.wipo.int.

Obtaining protection is only half the battle. To win the war in keeping your IP safe, you must be vigilant to protect your rights, making sure that someone does not steal them out from under you. Here are some steps to follow:

1. Monitor regularly the use of your IP. For example, Google your trademark to see if anyone is using it without your permission. Search for sales of items made with your patented concepts.

2. Send a cease and desist letter. Contact any violators to put them on notice that they are infringing your protected property. Often violators do not steal your intellectual property intentionally and will readily comply with your warning to stop using your property. Have an IP attorney draft a form letter for you that you can then send to violators. The initial cost of the attorney's work in this matter is well worth it.

3. File a civil action if a violator will not stop after your warning. If your civil action is successful, the violator will be prohibited from further use of your intellectual property and liable to you for monetary damages (e.g., any profits the violator received through the illegal use of your IP).

4. Inform government authorities of violations. They may pursue criminal charges against violators, such as for counterfeiting and piracy.

To learn more about what you can do to obtain and maintain IP protection, go to www.stopfakes.gov/smallbusiness. Or call (866) 999-HALT to speak with an IP attorney who can answer questions and, where appropriate, direct you to other government resources, such as the Department of Justice or the Department of Homeland Security.

Contracts and Agreements

In the old days, a handshake and a person's word were as solid as stone tablets. In today's commercial arena, we rely on written agreements. The purpose of having a contract is to set forth the terms and conditions of a deal clearly, concisely, and completely so that both parties know what's expected. Basic information to be included in any contract is a description of the parties—legal names and addresses, a description of the goods or services to be provided, and the price and payment terms (e.g., on delivery).

Making It Legal

A contract does not have to be written in complicated legalese or contain pages and pages of boilerplate clauses (although some of these clauses are helpful) to be an effective binding agreement. But some boilerplate clauses are commonly used by lawyers to save time while ensuring the contract meets your needs. Some helpful boilerplate clauses include:

- *Governing law.* Specify which state's laws govern the terms of the contract, a necessary provision when you are contracting with someone in another state (or who may later be in another state).

- *Severability.* This clause keeps the contract in force even if one or more clauses are later invalid.

Where required, make sure the contract is in writing. For example, you cannot enforce a contract for the sale of goods over $500, a contract that takes more than one year to perform, or one for the sale of real property unless you have a written agreement. Remember that any of the terms and conditions discussed among the parties before or during the course of drafting an agreement are displaced by the terms of a written contract. So if you thought the parties had agreed to a price of $1,000, but the contract says $1,500, $1,500 is the price to be paid.

Mediation and Arbitration Clauses

Despite your best intentions and an airtight contract, it's inevitable that problems will arise at some time. To avoid the need for costly court action, it's helpful to include a mediation or arbitration clause in your contracts. This mandates that both parties agree to use mediation or arbitration to resolve a conflict. Using mediation or arbitration is faster and less costly than litigation.

Mediation is a process in which a neutral third party works with parties to the contract to try to reach a consensus.

Arbitration is a process in which a neutral third party acts like a judge to dictate a result that both parties to the contract agree in advance to follow. Unlike a court decision, however, there is no appeal from the arbiter's ruling.

Amending Contracts

Often, during the course of operations, the contract you so carefully worked out no longer suits the situation. The contract should be changed to adapt to new circumstances. The process of amending a contract is the same as for writing the original contract. Use all the same care and formalities that went into the original contract in order to continue legal protections.

The following subsections give you some special guidance on certain types of written agreements—points to include and other rules to follow.

Sales Contracts

If you sell goods, a contract is advisable to spell out the terms of sale. Include a description of what you are selling and the price. Also include any additional terms, such as service agreements or warranties, discounts for prompt payment, and delivery terms.

Service Contracts

If you perform services, a contract is advisable to protect you and ensure that you are paid for your work. Terms of the contract should include:

- *Description of the work to be performed.* Depending on the nature of the job, this may include a timetable for performance.

- *Payment terms,* including the amount to be paid and when partial payments are due.

- *Obligation to pay expenses.* Travel expenses and job materials usually are included in the price of a service contract, but spell out details for these and other expenses.

- *Termination rights.* Usually each party retains the right to terminate the contract under set circumstances. Detail what these circumstances are and how to terminate the contract (e.g., 30 days' notice in writing).

- *Any other important terms.* If you are an independent contractor, this status usually is included in a service contract.

Leases

Renting commercial space is not like signing a lease for a personal apartment. There are many terms and conditions to commercial leases. Unlike consumer leases, there are no stock commercial lease forms; most terms of the lease are negotiated and reflected in the final lease agreement. Points to consider in a commercial lease include:

- *Lease term*—how long the initial lease period runs and whether there are renewal periods.

- *Rent*—including initial rent and future rent increases ("escalations") and how these increases are figured. Some commercial leases adjust annually. Where there are sizable property tax increases and fuel costs, the annual rent increase may be substantial. A company that provides virtual office space in a high-rise in a New York suburb, where its tenants pay by the hour, day, or month, experienced a more than 23 percent increase in rent in 2005 because of these factors.

- *What the rent includes.* With a net lease, you may pay insurance and property taxes separately from the rental amount. With a gross lease, these additional costs are part of the rental amount.

- *Who is responsible*—for maintenance (ordinary repairs such as painting) and improvements (capital expenditures such as fixtures and permanent partitions).

- *Other terms*, including sublease rights, termination conditions, and arbitration/mediation requirements to settle disputes.

Employment Agreements

For small businesses, this is usually a letter offering a position to an employee. The letter details all of the terms of the job, including job title, salary, starting date, and so on. Be sure to include a statement that the employee is an "at will" employee. This allows you to terminate the employee at any time for any reason; no misbehavior or cause is required for termination. Of course, the employee retains the right to quit at any time as well. Also include a requirement that the employee agrees to sign confidentiality agreements. The letter to the employee should close with a statement that the terms contained in it are the entire agreement of the parties. It can be amended only in writing, signed by both parties.

When you engage independent contractors, you should also use similar agreements. Specify that the parties agree to an independent contractor relationship and that the contractor understands his or her responsibility for taxes.

Confidentiality Agreements

Companies often have proprietary information, including customer lists, products that are in development (and have not yet been patented), and other confidential assets. In order to protect them, make sure employees and any third parties you share information with agree to keep your information confidential.

For example, say you are developing a special marketing process and want to show what you've done so far to an expert. Before revealing *anything*, have that person sign a confidentiality agreement. Then, if that person should use your process in violation of the agreement, you have a legal basis for seeking redress. Usually, confidentiality agreements contain a clause authorizing injunctive relief so that you can get a court to order the other party to cease using your process immediately. This does not negate your rights to seek damages for the time that the process was in use.

Promissory Notes

A promissory note is an IOU for a loan. If you borrow or lend money in the course of your business, including loans between you and the company, be sure to put the terms of the loan in writing with a promissory note. Points to include in a promissory note are:

- *Borrowed amount.* Specify the principal of the loan.

- *Interest rate.* Set the amount of interest, if any, that is owed by the borrower.

- *Repayment terms.* Fix the repayment schedule (weekly, monthly, annually) or other repayment terms, such as on demand or ballooning at a future date on which all of the funds must be repaid in a lump sum. If the terms are interest only, with principal due at the end of a set term, make this arrangement clear.

- *Security.* Specify whether there is any security for the loan.

- *Other terms.* Also specify that the failure to enforce the note when the borrower misses a payment is not an admission that an amount has been forgiven or that the other terms of the note are void.

Saving Money

You can cut down on attorney's fees by preparing draft agreements yourself and then paying counsel only to review your work. The more legwork you do, the less it will cost you when you meet with an attorney. Once an attorney has reviewed one type of contract, you can then make minor changes or corrections for future use without additional legal review. For example, have your attorney review a standard sales contract and then use it with future customers, merely changing the party's information, terms of sale, and other variables.

To find some online agreements that you can purchase for a modest fee (e.g., $25) or download for free and then tailor for your situation, go to AllBusiness (www.allbusiness.com and click on "Forms & Agreements"), LawDepot.com (www.lawdepot.com and click on "Document Center"), and Nolo (www.nolo.com/index.cfm and click on "Business & Human Resources").

Know the Law

You may have heard the expression that ignorance of the law is no excuse—you can wind up in trouble if you fail to learn about your responsibilities. For example, it is vital that you understand labor laws so you don't inadvertently violate them by failing to pay required overtime or by using discriminatory hiring practices. Your best protection is to educate yourself on your legal obligations.

Fortunately, the Internet can connect you to many valuable resources on a variety of topics to help you learn about the law and your responsibilities.

RESOURCES

Here are some important places to look for help in learning about the law and your responsibilities:

- E-legal.com (www.e-legal.com) for free legal advice on many business topics, including contracts, intellectual property, and employment issues.

- Internal Revenue Service (www.irs.gov/businesses/small/index.html) to find an online classroom that will explain your federal tax obligations, including income and employment taxes.

- LawInfo.com (www.lawinfo.com) for free legal advice on many business topics, including business law, intellectual property, and workers' compensation.

- Nolo—Law for All (www.nolo.com and click on "Business and Human Resources") for featured articles and topics such as buying or selling a business and human resources.

- U.S. Department of Labor (www.dol.gov and click on "Employers") to find information about wages (including minimum wage and FairPay overtime rules), work hours, workplace safety, looking for job applicants, and free workplace posters you are required to display.

- WorldLawDirect.com (www.worldlawdirect.com and click on "Business Law") for frequently asked questions (FAQs) on various topics.

Buy-Sell Agreements

All of the contracts and agreements discussed thus far in this chapter concern your dealings with third parties (customers, clients, suppliers, creditors, etc.). But it is also important to have an agreement among owners of your company to decide what happens in case one co-owner is no longer in the picture for any number of reasons, including death. In small businesses, owners usually want to keep things among themselves and not give spouses, children, or outsiders ownership interests. For instance, if one owner dies, a spouse may inherit stock in the business and become an owner, with all the rights of those who founded the business and work in it on a daily basis. In order to keep ownership between intended parties, it is wise to use a buy-sell agreement.

A buy-sell agreement can be used by co-owners to specify what happens to the interests of one owner when he or she wants to leave the business, becomes disabled, retires, goes bankrupt, divorces, or, most significantly, dies. There are two main types of buy-sell agreements:

1. *A cross-purchase agreement* in which the remaining owner or owners buy out the interest of the departing owner.

2. *A stock redemption agreement* in which the corporation buys back the departing owner's interest. This is accomplished by having the corporation redeem the stock from the departing owner (or his or her estate).

A hybrid agreement combines both main types, with the corporation redeeming a portion of the stock and the remaining shareholder or shareholders buying the balance from the departing shareholder.

Writing up a buy-sell agreement and signing it is only half the battle. In order to win the war you must have adequate funding in place to pay for the terms of the agreement. Typically, life insurance is used to fund the agreement in the event of death because it assures sufficient money on hand when needed and it may not cost too much to carry the insurance. The ownership of the policy depends on the type of agreement in place. With a cross-purchase agreement, each owner carries insurance on the lives of the other owners.

For example, say there are three co-owners of a limited liability company whom we'll call Adam, Beth, and Chuck. Adam has policies on Beth's and Chuck's lives. Beth has policies on

Adam's and Chuck's lives. And Chuck has policies on Adam's and Beth's lives. This is a total of six policies. If Chuck dies, both Adam and Beth collect on their policies and use the funds to satisfy their obligation under the buy-sell agreement to buy out Chuck's interest.

With a stock redemption agreement, the corporation carries a policy on the lives of each shareholder. In the example, if the business were a corporation rather than an LLC, the corporation would carry life insurance coverage on Adam's, Beth's, and Chuck's lives, for a total of three policies. If Chuck dies, the corporation uses the life insurance proceeds to redeem his shares from his estate.

Which type of agreement is better to use? It depends on your situation. Obviously, it is easier to work with a stock redemption agreement since the business is buying and paying for the insurance. Thus, even if the owners are different ages or sexes or have different health histories, all of which affect premium costs, the cost of coverage through the corporation is shared more equally. In contrast, in a cross-purchase agreement, one owner may pay more for coverage on another's life when these factors differ. However, it may be possible to simplify insurance coverage by using a "first-to-die" policy covering all of the owners' lives. In this instance, one policy is used, with the cost of premiums shared by owners.

With multiple owners, cross-purchase agreements can become complex, requiring numerous life insurance policies. However, if the business is a partnership or a limited liability company, the cross-purchase agreement may be the only alternative.

And there are tax consequences to these alternatives. In a stock redemption agreement, the corporation can deduct the cost of insuring the owners. In a cross-purchase agreement, co-owners cannot deduct the premiums they paid, even though it could be argued that this is a business expense. But they get a stepped-up basis for the interest they buy with the insurance proceeds.

There is another important use for buy-sell agreements, in addition to securing ownership rights for remaining owners. Properly drafted buy-sell agreements can be used to fix the value of a deceased owner's interest for estate tax purposes.

Funding Other Events

Life insurance is usually used only for funding buyouts at death. But owners may depart for any number of other reasons. It is important to work out other funding mechanisms for these events, such as using company profits to pay off those who succeed to the parting owner's interest. For instance, if a divorce court awards an owner's interest (or portion of that interest) to a divorcing spouse, the business can use profits to buy out that interest and keep the spouse from becoming an ongoing owner.

According to statistics from the National Association of Insurance Commissioners and UnumProvident Corporation, a company with two partners, both age 35, has a 67 percent chance that one of the partners will suffer a disability of three months or longer before reaching age 65. It may be possible to use special insurance, called a disability buyout policy. This coverage is *not* the same as a typical disability policy that provides income when an owner becomes disabled. Instead, the buyout policy pays a lump sum at once or over a period (typically two to five years) that can be used to buy out the disabled owner's interest. Because one in seven people will be disabled for at least five years before reaching age 65 (according to the American Council of Life Insurers), it may be advisable to explore this funding mechanism for your buy-sell agreement.

Check the terms of the agreement carefully. Most, for example, will not pay anything before 12 to 24 months to ensure that in fact there is a disability preventing the owner from returning to work. Since these policies can be expensive, consider longer waiting periods and installment payments to lower premiums.

LESSONS ABOUT PROTECTING YOURSELF

✔ Set up your business to afford you personal liability protection if your line of work requires it.

✔ Take legal steps to protect your business's intellectual property assets.

✔ Use written contracts and agreements with third parties to protect your interests.

✔ If you write your own contracts and agreements, have them reviewed by an attorney just to be safer.

✔ Learn the law, because ignorance of it is no excuse.

✔ Use buy-sell agreements among co-owners to protect ownership interests in the event of death, disability, divorce, retirement, or bankruptcy.

Carry Enough Insurance

Protection is not a principle but an expedient.
—Benjamin Disraeli

*T*hings happen—*property gets damaged, an employee is injured, goods are stolen. Very large corporations may have the financial resources to withstand these events, but small businesses must rely on deeper pockets than their own for protection—through adequate insurance. The types of insurance and extent of protection you require depend in part on the nature of your business. Those that are labor intensive may spend more money on employee-related insurance than manufacturers that need other types of coverage.*

In deciding on the coverage to carry, weigh your needs against the cost of premiums, keeping in mind what your exposure may be in case of an insurable event, such as a fire or discrimination claim against you. If you think you need a certain type of coverage, then find a way to pay for it. The more insurance you carry, the greater your ability to withstand events that befall you.

In this chapter you will see how to assess the kinds of insurance you may wish to carry. Some insurance coverage is mandatory by law or contract, while other coverage is discretionary. You'll find out important details about key types of coverage. And you'll learn about ways in which to cut insurance costs.

Kinds of Insurance

There are many different types of coverage. Some of them are mandatory (e.g., you must pay for workers' compensation if you have employees) or essential, such as a business owner's package, (BOP) policy to cover liability and property damage. You have more discretion with other types of coverage, such as employer liability protection insurance to cover you from actions including wrongful termination suits.

The following provides a brief description of each type of coverage and whether it is mandatory. Some of these types are discussed in greater detail throughout this chapter.

Accident and health coverage. This is medical coverage for yourself and staff, including spouses and dependents. Pending legislation would mandate coverage in the state of Washington for companies with more than 50 employees. California voters narrowly rejected in November 2004 a proposition mandating coverage for companies with 200 or more employees starting in 2006 (50 employees starting in 2007). Health coverage is discussed later in this chapter.

Automobile insurance. If the company owns a car and/or a truck, you are required to carry liability and collision coverage to pay for damages your vehicle may cause to others. If you lease the vehicle, make sure the policy includes "gap coverage" for the difference between what is owed on the lease and what the car's value is should it be stolen or totaled.

Business interruption insurance. This gives you cash during a period in which the business is forced to close because of a natural disaster or civil unrest. The money is used to pay ongoing costs, such as rent and employee wages, as well as rent and related expenses in temporary facilities (see later in this chapter). While this coverage is *not* mandatory, it is highly advisable. Think about the businesses in the Gulf region that wish they had this coverage following Hurricane Katrina.

Business owner's package (BOP) policy. This provides comprehensive coverage for both liability and property damage for small businesses.

Casualty insurance. Obtain reimbursement for property damage caused by floods, fires, and other destructive events. Casualty insurance usually is combined with liability coverage under a comprehensive business owner's package (BOP) policy discussed later in this chapter. While this coverage is *not* mandatory, it is highly advisable.

Credit insurance. If you sell goods on credit, consider this coverage for nonpayment of debts owed to your business.

Cyber coverage. If you have a web site, consider protection from claims arising from your content. For example, you may have exposure for copyright violation.

Directors and officers (D&O) insurance. Protect yourself from personal liability for errors you may make in a management capacity. This coverage is distinct from errors and omissions (E&O) coverage that protects against performance failures and negligence in connection with your company's products or services. D&O is limited to acts of management.

Disability insurance. When a physical or mental impairment prevents you or an employee from working, this coverage pays a set monthly amount to replace a portion of lost wages. The injury need not be job-related (as in the case of workers' compensation). While this coverage is *not* mandatory, it is highly advisable at least for yourself and is discussed later in this chapter.

Employment practices liability insurance (EPLI). Protection in case of claims arising from employees, including wrongful termination, sexual harassment, or discrimination practices. The need for this type of coverage grows with the size of your staff, although these types of actions are becoming more prevalent. Expect to pay $2,000 or more annually for $1 million in protection.

Errors and omissions (E&O) insurance. Similar to professional liability coverage discussed below, this policy protects you for doing or failing to do something in your line of work. Self-employed individuals carry this coverage to protect themselves. Companies carry the coverage for protection from the acts of employees.

Key-person life insurance. If you or another owner or key employee dies, this can adversely affect the business. For protection, have the company carry life insurance to pay for the search for a replacement and to cover any losses until a qualified person can be found.

Kidnap and ransom coverage. A relatively new type of policy provides protection that is helpful for business owners who travel

abroad. Corporate policies cover such expenses as hostage negoti-
ation fees, lost wages to you or your employee who has been kid-
napped, and, most importantly, the ransom amount.

Life insurance. Various types of life insurance arrangements are
used in a business context. Usually, life insurance is carried on the
lives of owners as a funding mechanism for buy-sell agreements
(i.e., to buy out the deceased owner's interest). Some owners use
split-dollar life insurance arrangements in which the cost of personal coverage is shared with the business (although recent tax
rule changes make these arrangements less attractive). Some companies may offer life insurance as a fringe benefit to employees,
usually in the form of group-term coverage.

Overhead insurance. Similar to business interruption coverage,
this type of policy pays rent, salaries, and other overhead expenses
during periods of an owner's illness.

Pension Benefit Guaranty Corporation (PBGC) coverage. If
your business has a defined benefit retirement plan, you must
pay premiums to the Pension Benefit Guaranty Corporation
(www.pbgc.gov), a quasi-federal agency, to protect employee pensions in the event your plan fails. For 2005, the annual premium
was $19 per participant, plus a variable rate charge if your plan is
underfunded ($9 per $1,000 of underfunded benefits). But pending legislation would hike the basic annual premiums substantially (58 percent to $30 per year under the House version and 146
percent to $46.75 under the Senate version). Presumably, any pre-
mium hike would apply starting in 2006.

Performance bonds. While not technically insurance, you may
be required to secure this coverage to guarantee the faithful performance of employees' and/or the business's performance on a
contract. While not mandated by law, performance bonds are usually a condition of a construction contract. For more details, see the
description of surety bonds.

Product liability coverage. If you sell or manufacture products,
this coverage protects you from claims arising from defects in the
products that cause injuries to the public. Again, the law does not
require you to carry the coverage, but you may have to do so as a
condition for selling your products. For instance, if you market
health remedies, your local pharmacy won't stock your items unless you furnish evidence of product liability coverage.

Professional liability coverage. Also called malpractice insurance, this coverage protects doctors, lawyers, accountants, and other professionals from claims arising out of their professional duties. Even if professionals incorporate their practices or form limited liability partnerships (LLPs), the entity does not protect them from malpractice claims.

Surety bonds. These act as guarantees to third parties that you will do what you claim or promise to do. For example, if you have employees, you can protect the business from third-party claims arising from employee actions, such as theft from a customer's home during the course of a job.

There are different types of surety bonds, including:

- *Bid bonds.* If you bid on contracts, this type of bond assures the party requesting the bids that you will execute the contract if you are the lowest bidder and win the contract; if you fail to execute the contract, the amount of the bond goes to the other party. Typically, bid bonds run about 10 percent of the contract amount and are usually required for all public sector projects as well as some private projects.

- *Dishonesty bonds.* Also called fidelity bonds, these protect third parties from the dishonest acts of your employees. Typically, these bonds are carried by cleaning companies to provide protection to customers against employee theft. They provide blanket coverage for all employees, regardless of the number of hours they work.

- *License bonds.* Typically, licensed contractors are required to post a bond guaranteeing that they can perform certain types of work within set parameters.

- *Performance bonds.* These guarantee that you will complete the work as promised. If you were required to post a bid bond, expect to need a performance bond (usually within 30 days of the contract award). The cost of the bond depends on the contract price, type of work involved, and your background. Typically, a bond's premium can range from 1 percent to 4 percent of the contract price.

- *Payment (or final) bonds.* These guarantee that everyone supplying labor and materials to a project will be paid. Typically they are part and parcel of performance bonds and are included in their cost; it is very rare that a payment-only bond is required.

A surety bond is issued by a surety company, which functions much like an insurance company. It assesses the probability of your being able to fulfill your obligations so that it will not be called upon to pay out to third parties.

To obtain coverage, typically you must provide three years of financial statements showing work in progress, accounts payable, accounts receivable, and bank references. There may be simplified applications for bonds under $100,000.

If you have difficulty obtaining a bond because you've been in business only a short time or for some other reason, check out the Small Business Administration's Office of Surety Guarantees (www.sba.gov/osg). While the SBA does not *issue* bonds directly, it provides a *guarantee* for bid, performance, and payment bonds. Contracts up to $2 million can qualify for the SBA bond guarantee.

Unemployment coverage. This coverage protects employees from complete loss of income due to involuntary terminations (other than for serious cause). Coverage is mandated by federal and state law. Federal unemployment coverage is collected as an employment tax under the Federal Unemployment Tax Act (FUTA). States also levy insurance based on a company's unemployment claims experience (the more employees who collect, the higher the company's premiums). Self-employed individuals cannot obtain unemployment insurance since they are not employees.

Workers' compensation. If you have employees you must provide this coverage, which pays benefits for injuries incurred in the course of employment.

Business Owner's Package Policy

The basic insurance needs of every business include protection from liability (e.g., a customer's injury on your premises) and property damage (e.g., a fire destroys the contents of your location). Coverage can be purchased separately, but it is most common for small businesses to buy a business owner's package (BOP) policy to cover both contingencies. While the law does not require you to carry this coverage as a condition of doing business, it is the most basic form of protection. Buy the best policy you can afford.

A BOP is a comprehensive policy that provides protection for named perils, such as theft; it does not cover acts of professional negligence or errors and omissions by officers and directors (separate coverage for these occurrences are explained in the preceding section). More specifically, it provides coverage for:

- Damage to physical assets that you own or lease, including inventory (perishable and nonperishable) and equipment.

- Theft, including so-called inventory shrinkage due to shoplifting and employee theft of merchandise (according to the FBI, retailers annually experience about $30 billion in losses).

- Accidents that result in bodily claims by third parties (e.g., customers) as well as damage to their property and claims for libel, slander, and false advertising.

A BOP can be structured to include business interruption coverage discussed shortly. Usually BOPs are limited to businesses with fewer than 100 employees and annual revenue below $1 million. When the company grows larger, a comprehensive policy is no longer used.

The premiums you pay depend on many factors, including the type of business you are in, the length of time you have been in business, and the time you have been at your current location. For instance, any type of business that involves ladders (e.g., painting contractors) will pay significantly higher premiums than more staid occupations.

Special Consideration for Home-Based Businesses

Don't assume your homeowner's policy will protect your business-related losses. Your homeowner's policy may provide only limited coverage for property damage and may not cover liability for business guests, as one self-employed accountant working from home in Baltimore found out when a client fell on her front steps and sustained a serious facial injury. You can gain adequate protection by purchasing a separate BOP. However, depending on your situation, it may be less costly and just as effective to modify your homeowner's policy. For instance, if you rarely have customers to your home, add a rider to your existing policy for liability protection for business guests. Up personal property protection for computer systems and other business equipment not regularly covered under the policy.

Business Interruption Insurance

The American Red Cross reports that as many as 40 percent of small businesses never reopen following a flood, tornado, earthquake, or other disaster. One reason for the failure to survive is the lack of funds to keep going. The best solution to ensure the continued viability of your business is carrying adequate business interruption insurance (BII). You can bet that many a small-business owner on the Gulf Coast or in Florida wished there was such insurance in place following Hurricanes Katrina, Rita, and Wilma in 2005.

Business interruption insurance usually provides money to pay ongoing expenses (e.g., payroll, utilities, rent, etc.) when your business is suspended because of a disaster. It can also compensate you for lost profits (the money you would have earned if the disaster had not struck, based on your financial records). And it can pay for extra expenses you may incur to keep going, such as rent in a temporary location and overtime wages to make up for lost time.

BII usually does not pay for property damage; your property insurance policy covers this loss. However, BII is often sold as an endorsement to a property insurance policy or the two policies are sold as a package.

Caution: You may carry BII but not have the protection you think you have. Make sure that:

- *Coverage applies to all disasters you anticipate.* Your policy might exclude certain disasters, such as floods, earthquakes, and windstorms. Check for coverage in case of a terrorist attack. Buy an all-risk policy if you can afford it, rather than a named-peril policy that only covers certain events, such as fire. But even with an all-risk policy, you may have to *add* perils, such as flood coverage underwritten by the federal flood insurance program.

(Even if you are not in a high-risk flood plain, it may be wise to carry this additional coverage for floods caused by high rains or other events.) Check whether your business owner's package (BOP) policy provides any BII and whether it is adequate for your needs.

- *Benefits are paid when you think they should be.* Most policies pay when there is a business "suspension." If you're shut down completely because your property is damaged or destroyed, there is usually no issue. But if you experience a substantial loss of business because of a disaster (e.g., you were a block away from ground zero on 9/11), will your policy protect you?

- *Benefits are sufficient to sustain your business.* The policy may limit coverage to a set period (the "period of restoration"), but it may take you longer to get back in business and you will want the policy to continue payments for this additional period. *Note:* Also check the waiting period before benefits will start (e.g., 48 hours), so that you have a cash cushion to tie you over this time.

Cost of Coverage

Cost is always a factor in deciding on insurance coverage. Don't try to buy a policy that meets 100 percent of your needs in case of loss; it is just too expensive. More realistically, consider insuring for 80 percent of your anticipated needs. This will probably cost annually around 2 percent of the amount you are insuring. For example, if your policy covers 80 percent of the $12,000 you normally need every month for operating expenses and profits, your annual BII premium would be around $2,300 ($12,000 × 80% × 2% × 12).

Workers' Compensation

Workers' compensation protects your employees if they are injured on the job. Premiums for this coverage are based on many factors, including your industry, location, and claims experience. You have *no* control over your industry, little control over your location (you're not likely to relocate solely because of workers' compensation premiums), but substantial control over claims experience. Here are some steps to take that can reduce your premiums.

Make Safety a Priority

This means focusing time, attention, *and* money on creating policies and procedures to reduce accidents and injuries on the job. Use a commonsense approach to correcting safety problems. For example, restaurants statistically have a high rate of slip-and-fall injuries; requiring workers to wear sneakers or other rubber-soled shoes can reduce these incidents.

There may be many no-cost or low-cost actions you can take to cut claims and reduce premiums. For example, if your workers are experiencing repetitive stress injuries, something as simple as rotating assignments can help avoid problems. If your workers may be subject to back injuries from heavy lifting, suggest lifting methods that will help them avoid back problems.

Make sure workers know your policies and procedures. Use employee safety manuals, training seminars, and posters to educate your workforce.

Work Closely with Your Insurance Agent

Insurance will be paid out to injured workers only if you have insured them correctly. This means clearly telling the agent what workers do in order that they can be properly classified. If they are misclassified, your insurance may be canceled and it can be difficult to obtain new coverage.

Watch for employee fraud in making claims. It pays to track down suspicious claims and help insurance companies fight them so premiums won't be increased.

Ask for Help

Contact a safety expert to review your workplace and make recommendations on how to improve safety. The cost of the expert may be less than the fines you could be charged for safety violations and can help to reduce your workers' compensation premiums.

Use resources available through the Occupational Safety and Health Administration (OSHA). You are entitled to a *free* consultation to identify safety and health hazards in your workplace. For general information on OSHA assistance to small businesses, go to www.osha.gov/Publications/osha3163.pdf.

Get Workers Back on the Job

Accidents may happen, but the sooner you encourage injured workers to return to work, the smaller your claims and the lower your premiums will be. Doing this may require you to work with outside human resources (HR) consultants to manage employee cases if this is not part of your insurance coverage.

Idea: Allow returning workers to assume a lighter workload or use reduced hours to get them back on the job.

Relocate

This is a drastic step, but moving to an area that offers a number of benefits, including low workers' compensation premiums, can save you big dollars. (See Table 11.1.) Investigate carefully all the ramifications of a move before investing any money toward this end.

TABLE 11.1   States with Least Expensive Workers' Compensation Premiums

1. North Dakota	6. Utah
2. Indiana	7. Massachusetts
3. Arizona	8. Kansas
4. Arkansas	9. Iowa
5. Virginia	10. Oregon and South Carolina

Source: Small Business Survival Index 2005, Small Business & Entrepreneurship Council, October 2005.

Unemployment Insurance

If you have employees, you pay a premium (essentially a tax) to your state that provides unemployment benefits when employees are laid off (only Alaska imposes an unemployment tax on workers themselves). You also pay federal unemployment tax (FUTA). The rate you pay to your state is based on your experience, that is, the claims that are made against you by laid-off workers (new employers are assigned an initial rate that is adjusted later to reflect experience). The fewer the unemployment claims, the lower your premiums (tax rate) will be. Here are ways in which to minimize your state unemployment insurance premiums:

Think Before You Hire (So You Won't Have to Fire)

If you terminate a worker because business is slow, the worker is probably eligible for benefits (a claim against you). Before you increase your staff, make sure you're in a position to make a long-term commitment. Consider using alternative hiring arrangements, including temporary workers, before hiring permanent staff.

Do everything possible to make sure any employee you do hire will work out. Take as much time as you need during the hiring process to verify that the employee is a good match for your business; check employment history carefully.

Pay Premiums Only on Taxable Wages

Generally, the rate you pay to your state unemployment fund is applied to taxable wages. This is a specific term; some amounts you think are taxable may be excludable under your state's definition. Excludable wages include, for example, the value of employee discounts, facilities or privileges (e.g., entertainment); supper money; and payments for sickness after six months. In figuring FUTA taxes, be sure to claim the appropriate credit for state premiums.

Review Claims for Errors

When a terminated worker applies for benefits, make sure you're the employer responsible for paying them. Usually, the most recent employer is charged with benefits to the extent of certain wages (or, in the state of Washington, an employee's hours). If the claim names you but the employee hasn't worked for you recently, there may be a mistake.

Also check the amount of the claim. Someone who worked for you at a modest pay rate may be collecting too much in benefits.

Finally, check the reason given for unemployment. If the employee left voluntarily, a claim for benefits may be unfounded. To see how much an unemployment claim can cost you, go to www.adp.com/taxfin/toolbox/unemployment/calculator.asp.

Contest Unfounded Claims

Not all employees who leave your company are entitled to benefits, even if they apply for them. Yes, it's time-consuming, but be sure to file an appeal to a grant of benefits if you believe it isn't appropriate. Generally, benefits should not be given if the worker:

- Left voluntarily (e.g., for a better job).

- Was fired for gross misconduct in connection with work.

- Changed job status from full-time at another company to part-time at yours. (Partial benefits may be collected, but the part-time employer isn't responsible for them.)

Watch time limits for contesting a determination. For example, you may have only two weeks to act before you lose the opportunity to challenge a grant of benefits that results in a claim against you.

For rules on contesting claims, check with your state unemployment department. Find yours by going to www.doleta.gov/programs/uimap.asp?483,205.

Health Insurance

Health insurance costs are high and only going higher. Despite the cost, the majority of small businesses offer such coverage; 52 percent of businesses with nine or fewer employees had health coverage in 2004 (according to a Kaiser Family Foundation annual survey). If you want coverage for yourself or you want to offer employees coverage as a way to compete with larger employers, explore your health coverage choices and ways to minimize costs. Health insurance can be supplemented or supplanted by other health insurance arrangements to provide broad coverage at lower cost.

Factors in Plan Selection

The factors you should use in selecting the best medical plan for your business include:

- *Cost (medical insurance and health plan contributions).* Which type of health coverage should you carry? Who should pay for coverage—the business, your employees, or both? Today, 80 percent of employees with self-only coverage and 90 percent with family coverage contribute to premium payments.

- *Convenience (managing a health plan, including administration of disbursements).* Who sets up and runs the plan and decides on whether disbursements should be made?

- *Employee morale (account portability and flexibility).* What happens to funds in health accounts at the end of the year? What can funds be used for?

Health Coverage Alternatives

You have a wide range of options. Your choice naturally depends in great part on cost.

TRADITIONAL HEALTH COVERAGE

This is the Cadillac of coverage, where the insurer pays for claims—usually there are modest deductibles and co-payments (e.g., $15 per office visit). This coverage can take various forms, including health maintenance organizations (HMOs) that require all care be funneled through a primary care provider, preferred provider organizations (PPOs) that let you go directly to specialists, and point of service (POS) plans that provide greater flexibility for obtaining services outside of the company's network.

HEALTH SAVINGS ACCOUNTS (HSAs)

High-deductible (such as $1,050 or more) health insurance, which costs considerably less than traditional coverage, can be combined with savings-type accounts to pay for medicals costs not covered by the insurance. You can set up HSAs if you carry this type of coverage; companies have found that the high-deductible insurance plus contributions to employees' HSAs costs less than traditional health insurance alone. You don't have to contribute to employees' accounts, but if you do, this must be done on a nondiscriminatory basis. Funds contributed to an employee's account belong to the employee; he or she can take them and all the earnings when leaving employment. Contributions, which are limited by law, are fully deductible ($2,700 for an employee with individual coverage and $5,450 for an employee with family coverage in 2006, plus an additional $700 catch-up contribution permitted for anyone age 55 or older by the end of the year). Since employees own their accounts, you do not have to review claims submitted for reimbursement. It is up to each employee to keep track of the purpose of withdrawals by retaining receipts and other proof of medical treatment. Withdrawals for nonmedical reasons are permitted, but the funds are taxable to the employee and subject to a 10 percent penalty (unless the employee is disabled or eligible for Medicare). According to the National Small Business Association, a company with 15 employees, for example, that now has traditional health coverage could easily save 25 percent on health care costs by buying a high-deductible health policy and making contributions to employees' HSAs. For answers to questions on HSAs and insurance companies offering high-deductible coverage, go to www.hsainsider.com and www.hsafinder.com.

HEALTH REIMBURSEMENT ACCOUNTS (HRAs)

Typically this type of plan supplements other health coverage. HRAs are a bookkeeping entry account set up and funded entirely by a company on behalf of each employee. You decide how much to allot to each account every year (e.g., $1,000, $2,500, etc.); there is no limit fixed by law. Employees can then tap into these accounts to pay for medical costs not covered by insurance by submitting proof to you of a medical-related payment. No withdrawals from HRAs are permitted for nonmedical reasons. Amounts not used this year can be carried forward to pay medical costs in future years.

FLEXIBLE SPENDING ARRANGEMENTS (FSAs)

This type of plan can be used to shift the cost of coverage to employees who commit a fixed portion of their salaries to accounts created on their behalf. There is no contribution limit fixed by law; you set a limit in your FSA plan. Contributions are treated as salary reduction amounts (employees don't pay income tax on this portion of their wages). But amounts not used by the end of the year (or a grace period of up to two and a half months) are forfeited to the employer. Like HRAs, funds from FSAs can be used only for medical expenses; employees must submit to you proof of a medical-related payment. The arrangement can define the scope of eligible medical expenses.

Disability Insurance

The U.S. Census Bureau estimates that you have a 20 percent chance of becoming disabled for a long time as a result of an accident, illness, or debilitating condition. Your business may not survive without you. And you may not have the income needed to meet your personal expenses. You can deal with these contingencies with adequate insurance coverage.

Short-term disability coverage provided through state funds or company insurance generally runs only three to six months. You may be eligible for disability under Social Security, but payments from this source may not be adequate for your needs. You should carry long-term disability coverage to pay you a monthly benefit if you cannot work.

What you'll pay for this insurance depends not only on who you buy it from (discussed shortly), but also on:

- *How long benefits continue.* Payments continue for the period fixed in the policy—the longer this is, the higher the premiums. Generally, policies pay for 5 years, 10 years, or until you reach full retirement age for collecting Social Security benefits, assuming you remain disabled for this period.

- *Amount of monthly benefits.* The greater the benefits, the higher the premiums. Benefits under the policy are capped at a certain percentage of your regular monthly income (e.g., 50 percent or 66.67 percent).

- *Definition of disability.* The more liberal the definition, the higher the cost of the policy. For coverage in the event you are unable to perform the usual duties of your current occupation, you'll pay more than you would for coverage that will allow you to collect only if you cannot work at *any* job.

- *When benefits begin.* The longer you wait after becoming disabled to collect, the lower your premiums. For example, you'll pay more to collect after 31 days of disability than if you wait six months.

- *Inflation adjustment.* If your policy runs for many years (e.g., you buy one to cover you until you reach full retirement age), consider adding a cost-of-living feature that adjusts your benefits to reflect the impact of inflation. There is an additional cost for this feature.

- *Premium waiver.* Make sure the policy doesn't require you to pay premiums once disability has persisted for 90 days or longer (most policies automatically include this benefit).

Tax Issues

There are two tax-related considerations with disability insurance: whether premiums are deductible and whether benefits received under the policy are tax free. Understanding the tax rules and planning ahead can ensure the more favorable tax treatment.

PREMIUMS

If the business pays the premiums for your disability policy, it can deduct them. If you pay the premiums personally, you cannot deduct their cost. This is viewed as a nondeductible personal expense.

BENEFITS

If the business has paid the premiums and you collect benefits, you are taxed on them. If you paid the premiums and collect benefits, the benefits are tax free to you. There is no dollar limit to the amount of tax-free benefits you can receive. To protect your opportunity to receive tax-free benefits in the future, it is advisable that you pay the premiums, which can be facilitated by having the business increase its compensation to you. You'll pay taxes on the additional compensation, but this is less than the cost of the premiums. For example, if annual premiums are $1,200, you can receive additional compensation of $2,000 to cover this expense (assuming you are in a 40 percent combined federal and state tax bracket). The additional compensation only costs you $800 in taxes, leaving you $1,200 to pay the premium.

Equipment Maintenance Insurance

When you buy office equipment, a security or phone system, cash registers, medical equipment, or any other similar property, you are usually protected if things break down during a warranty period, typically 90 days or more. But in the past, if you wanted added protection, you had to buy an extended warranty contract or an equipment maintenance agreement.

Now there's an alternative: equipment maintenance insurance (EMI). While this type of coverage has been around for several years, it is underutilized by small businesses. You purchase insurance coverage that will pay for the cost of any repairs to your equipment. The insurance covers time and materials. In some instances, it may pay for the rental of a replacement unit (such as for 10 days) if the equipment has to be shipped out for servicing. The insurance runs for a one-year term and is renewable.

The advantages of EMI over an extended warranty include:

- *Simplicity.* You can use one EMI policy to cover *all* of your equipment. As the basic warranty on each item expires, you can roll coverage for that item into your insurance coverage. In contrast, each maintenance contract applies to a single piece of equipment that must be tracked individually to determine your coverage.

- *Cost.* Equipment maintenance insurance can run up to 20 percent less than the cost of a traditional maintenance contract. For example, Zurich, one of the leading carriers for this type of coverage, reviews your equipment, does a risk analysis, and then sets a premium that usually is more favorable to you than other protection.

- *Control.* You, and not the insurance company or another party, decide who should make the repairs and when. In contrast, repairs under maintenance agreements are usually handled by someone designated for this purpose (not necessarily someone you select).

Insurance Aspect

When the cost of repair exceeds the value of the equipment, at its option the insurance company may offer or extend a cash settlement. For instance, say you have a five-year-old photocopier that will cost $500 to repair. If its insured value is only $300, the insurance company will pay you the cash instead of repairing it. This cash can serve as a down payment on a new photocopier.

Cutting Insurance Costs

For some small businesses, insurance costs are a very significant part of the monthly budget. To the extent that costs can be trimmed, you can improve your bottom line. Here are some ways to help you reduce your insurance costs without cutting back on necessary coverage.

Shop Around

Different insurance carriers may charge different rates for the same protection. More often, however, for slight variations in premiums you may have very different levels of coverage. Get quotations from several insurance companies for each type of protection you are considering. As best you can, try comparing each policy feature by feature for an accurate cost comparison. For example, use the same dollar amount of coverage, the same deductible, and the same elimination period (the waiting period before coverage begins).

Cost isn't everything. You want a company that will pay

claims promptly and easily and are financially secure enough to provide needed protection in the future when claims arise. Check the rating of the insurance company through a rating service such as A. M. Best Company (www.ambest.com), Duff & Phelps (www.duffllc.com), Moody's Investors Service (www .moodys.com), Standard & Poor's (www.standardandpoors .com), or Weiss Ratings (www.weissratings.com). If you have any questions about a particular carrier, check with your state insurance department.

Special Considerations for Certain Types of Coverage

When comparison shopping for the type of health coverage you want, obtain free online insurance quotes from the following sites:

- 1StUSHealthquotes.com (www.ushealthquotes.com).

- HealthInsurance.com (www.eHealthInsurance.com).

- HealthInsuranceFinders.com (www.healthinsurancefinders.com and click on Group/Small Business Health Insurance).

- Insure.com (www.insure.com).

- MdInsuranceQuote.com (www.mdinsurancequote.com).

- Small Business Medical Insurance (www.small-business-medical-insurance.com).

For disability insurance, most major carriers offer the coverage, although Unum Life has nearly 30 percent of the market (www.disability.com). Other major carriers include MetLife (www.met.com), CIGNA (www.cigna.com), and Hartford Life (www.thehartford.com). Your company may obtain group rates if it buys or arranges the purchase of policies for all the owners and key employees of your business. You can buy a policy individually from an insurance company, but you may pay up to 10 times as much as you would for coverage under group insurance. You may also obtain more favorable (group) rates by buying coverage through a trade or professional association. It may be worth the annual association dues just for this benefit.

Work with a Knowledgeable Insurance Agent

A professional can help you assess your needs, find ways to cut costs, and, most importantly, secure coverage when underwriters are reluctant to issue a policy. Finding an insurance agent is discussed in Chapter 3.

Obtain Discounts

You may be eligible for premium reductions for a variety of reasons. For instance, if you have more than one policy with the same insurer, you may receive a multiple policy discount, which should be automatic. You may also receive discounts on property insurance for security systems, smoke detectors, and other safety devices.

Increase Deductibles

While you don't want to go "bare" (carry no coverage), you can substantially cut your premiums if you are willing to absorb a greater portion of any loss you sustain. View insurance as help for extraordinary, rather than ordinary, losses. For example, increasing the deductible from $500 to $1,000 may add only a modest exposure (an additional $500) for the business, but can cut premiums substantially.

Increase Elimination Periods

Like deductibles, the longer you wait for insurance to kick in, the lower your premiums will be. For instance, on business interruption coverage, instead of a 48-hour waiting period, consider a week or more. Similarly, extend the elimination period—say from one month to three or even six months—for disability coverage to reduce annual premiums.

Reduce the Need to Make Claims

The fewer claims you submit to the insurer for certain types of coverage, the lower your premiums will be. The best way to do this is not to refrain from submitting a claim when a loss occurs but rather to prevent the loss from occurring.

- Keep your premises safe to avoid accidents. Comply with Occupational Safety and Health Administration (OSHA) requirements and advice to avoid employee accidents (www.osha.gov). Take commonsense measures to keep customers safe as well. Educate employees on safe practices.

- Use devices or methods to safeguard property. Security systems with central alarm station monitoring can cut down on burglary or ensure a prompt response in case of fire. Use sound practices to store hazardous materials or substances.

- Make your products safe and reliable to avoid product liability claims.

Review Your Coverage Annually

Just because you found a good deal last year on a particular policy, do not assume you are as fortunate this year. Take the time to comparison shop again.

Making Insurance Claims

Having insurance does not automatically mean the company is standing ready to mail a check to you. In order to recover under a policy, you must take the appropriate steps to submit a claim. Depending on the policy and the insurer, this process can be simple or complex.

Making a claim usually requires documenting your losses. For example, under business interruption insurance, you need to prove your lost profits before the insurance company will pay you. To do this, you need adequate records, which can easily be destroyed in a disaster.

Safeguard Financial Records

It is highly advisable to store copies of your financial records offsite so that you can submit a substantiated claim when disaster strikes. For other safety precautions, see Chapter 12.

LESSONS ABOUT INSURING YOURSELF

✔ Determine what types of coverage you must or want to have.

✔ Carry a business owner's package (BOP) policy to gain broad coverage at modest rates.

✔ Carry business interruption coverage as a separate policy or as part of a BOP policy to pay expenses in case the business experiences a disaster.

✔ If you have employees, check for ways to minimize costs for workers' compensation and unemployment insurance.

✔ Explore your health care options and ways to minimize costs.

✔ Carry personal disability coverage in case you cannot work because of a physical or mental condition.

✔ Consider equipment maintenance insurance in lieu of extended warranties.

✔ Check for ways to minimize insurance costs.

✔ Understand the steps to take in submitting insurance claims.

Plan for Catastrophe and Disaster Recovery

If anything can go wrong, it will.
> —Murphy's Law (Captain Edward A. Murphy,
> an engineer working on Air Force Project
> MX981 at Edwards Air Force Base in 1949)

*D*isasters such as Hurricane Katrina are devastating events—both emotionally and financially—that are not easily overcome. If something happens to you, don't expect that things will ever get back to normal; they rarely do following a major disaster, according to the Public Entity Risk Institute (www.riskinstitute.org). The American Red Cross estimates that 40 percent of small businesses never recover from a disaster.

But you don't have to become a statistic and let disasters put you out of business. You can learn ways to protect yourself in order to minimize disaster exposure or its consequences. You can take action to get back to business as usual as quickly as possible.

In this chapter you will gain an understanding of the impact that a disaster can have on your business so that you become motivated to take action that can help you in the future. You will learn about disaster planning—the steps you can take to cushion yourself against both big and small unexpected events. Planning for your business includes procedures to follow if a storm or other event occurs, as well as directions to follow if something happens to you personally. You'll find out about special steps to take to protect your company's security. You'll also learn *about disaster recovery measures you can take to get back into business following a catastrophe.*

Your Reality Check on Disasters

Disasters can come about from natural causes, such as storms, earthquakes, and floods, from accidents, such as car accidents; or from just about any unplanned (unpleasant) event, such as power outages, riots, and terrorist attacks. Whatever the cause of the disaster, the result can be devastating to you and your business. Don't be complacent and think nothing will ever happen to you, because the statistics may prove you wrong. Consider these facts:

- Almost 10 percent of small business bankruptcies result from disasters and other calamities (U.S. Small Business Contract #SBA-95-0403 Paper, *Financial Difficulties of Small Businesses and Reasons for Their Failure*).

- Only 38 percent of small businesses have a disaster preparedness plan (NFIB Poll, 7/13/05 at www.nfib.com/object/IO_23694 .html).

- Some 30 percent of small businesses have been forced to shut their doors at least temporarily within the past three years because of a disaster (NFIB Poll, 7/13/05 at www.nfib.com/ object/IO_23694.html).

- Approximately 40 percent of small businesses never reopen following a flood, tornado, earthquake, or other disaster (American Red Cross at www.redcross.org/article/0,1072,0_332_1034,00 .html).

Insurance can certainly provide an important measure of protection, but usually goes only so far. For a discussion on key insurance to help you through a disaster, see Chapter 11.

It is interesting to note that some commercial lenders are now requiring businesses to have written disaster plans as a condition of granting a loan. The thinking is that unless you can recover from a disaster you won't be able to repay a loan. Some insurance companies are also imposing a similar requirement as a condition for issuing or renewing a policy. And we may see more demand for advance planning in light of Hurricane Katrina.

Disaster planning should entail a three-pronged attack:

1. *Prevention*—measures to avoid disasters where possible (e.g., keeping electrical lines safe to prevent fires).

2. *Disaster survival*—literally weathering the storm (e.g., heeding evacuation warnings).

3. *Recovery period*—steps for getting back to business (e.g., submitting insurance claims, making repairs, and reopening your doors for business).

Disaster Prevention

You can't affect the whims of Mother Nature to prevent blizzards, hurricanes, and earthquakes, but you can take actions that will minimize the possibility of certain types of disasters, such as fires and thefts.

Safety Checks

Any fire marshal will tell you that keeping aisles free of obstructions and minimizing clutter are simple but effective ways to avoid fires. Store your supplies and inventory safely.

If your business involves flammables or other hazardous materials such as paints and solvents, make sure to follow proper storage and removal procedures.

Electrical Checks

Check that electrical lines are not overloaded. For example, make sure appliances and machinery that draw a lot of current have sufficient electrical amperage (check manufacturer guidelines). Consider limiting employee use of radios, space heaters, and other electrical appliances that can short out or overload circuits, leading to fires.

Building Safety

Break-ins to stores, restaurants, and office buildings can result in theft or other problems. Review security measures for your building (and your space if you occupy a portion of a building). Include staff procedures for computer safety, such as logging off before leaving the premises at the end of the day. Work with an alarm company to secure your facilities where appropriate in order to dissuade break-ins by amateurs.

Create an Emergency Plan for Your Business to Weather the Storm

While September 11 may have made you acutely aware of what a terrorist attack can do to a business, and Hurricane Katrina has shown the impact of storms on business, other disasters—man-made or natural—can strike at any moment. Get the information you need to devise a plan to get you and your staff safely through a disaster. In making your plans, be especially sure to deal with the types of disaster you are most likely to face (for example, plan for flooding if you are located in a flood zone).

The objective of your plan is to get *through* the disaster with as little damage to persons and property as possible. Getting *over* the disaster and back to business can wait until later (and is discussed later in this chapter).

Getting Out

Another failure of the power grid on the East Coast will leave businesses in the area without electricity. Map out exit strategies from your building (taking into account the lack of elevator access). Include special planning for handicapped workers who need assistance. Like school fire drills, practicing escapes can help your staff become familiar with exits and evacuation procedures. Fix assembly areas where your staff can gather outside your building and account to you after an incident. Also learn about area evacuation routes for your town or city in case of hurricanes or other mandated evacuations.

Stock Up on Disaster Supplies

Think about what you and your staff would need to survive if a disaster requires you to remain in place (at your location). Water, nonperishable food, flashlights, extra batteries, and first-aid kits easily come to mind. But think beyond the obvious to be fully prepared—keep spare bulbs for the flashlight, a battery-operated radio to receive emergency instructions from local authorities, and a whistle for each worker to help emergency responders locate you. Advise your staff to think of their special needs (e.g., extra insulin and supplies for diabetics) and take measures to be prepared.

Special Equipment and Supplies

Depending on your business, you may need a backup generator (for example, to protect refrigerated goods) to see you through a disaster with minimal loss.

Supplies and Materials

There may be things you haven't even thought about that need to be addressed. For example, you could be indirectly affected by a disaster when your main supplier's facilities are wiped out. Or your usual shippers may experience problems. Supply chain planning—figuring out how you will get your supplies and materials and how you will get your wares to the public—will require some work and should be incorporated into your disaster planning.

Review Your Insurance Coverage

Check to see what types of natural and made-made disasters are (or are not) covered under your existing business policy. You may need to increase coverage if this option is available.

Think you're covered under your policy if a terrorist act damages your property or shuts you down? The events of September 11 may seem like ages ago, but the London subway bombings in 2005 are a fresher reminder that anything can happen just about anywhere. You may or may not have protection against these acts of violence. Check with your carrier for details on your coverage. Ask if there is any way to extend your protection if you think it is currently inadequate.

Educate Your Staff

Help employees think about what they would need if disaster strikes. This could include special medications and telephone contact information for children's schools or day care.

In addition to discussing at-work disaster plans, help your staff become prepared at home. If they know their families have things under control, your staff will be better able to focus on work and less likely to flee your premises if there is a disaster that may affect their children or other loved ones.

Work with Local Officials

Learn about area plans and resources for disasters. Some localities, for example, have developed special emergency response teams, and it would be wise to keep their contact information handy.

Resources for Creating a Disaster Plan

Unless you've gone through a disaster, you may not be able to envision all of the elements to include in your planning. Turn to experts for assistance in drafting your plan.

RESOURCES

Here are key disaster planning resources for you:

- Contact your local Red Cross chapter to attend a free seminar on risk management.

- Download "Preparing Your Business For the Unthinkable" from the American Red Cross (www.redcross.org/services/disaster/beprepared/busi_industry.html).

- Visit the Department of Homeland Security's web site (www.ready.gov/business/index.html) to learn about disaster planning. The site also explains what actions your business should take at different stages of the Homeland Security Advisory System. For example, at the orange (high) level, be alert to and report suspicious activities, contact vendors and suppliers to confirm their emergency plans, and determine the need to restrict access to your business or provide private security firm support).

Create an Emergency Plan for Your Absence

Surely every business owner is important to his or her company. But the smaller your business is, the more you need to think about what would happen to it if you are unable to work. Picture what happened to Tom's business when heart failure left him in the intensive care unit for four months. It was many weeks before he was even able to converse with his wife. He was confined to the hospital while awaiting a heart transplant and was laid up in recovery for a few months following successful surgery. Altogether, he was away from his company for 14 months. Could your business survive without you for this length of time?

Unlike large corporations, you don't have scores of officers and layers of personnel to continue running things seamlessly. Your incapacity—for a short period or a long term, from an accident or an illness—can derail your operations.

Your best survival strategy for others to carry on in your absence is to create an emergency plan. This is a written outline for action that your staff or family can follow to keep things running during a crisis.

Personnel Backup

If your personal services are vital to your operations—if you are a professional or skilled tradesperson—things won't run without you unless you've planned in advance for backup. Designate in your plan who should run things in your absence—an employee, your spouse, or someone else.

If you run a one-person business, you need to make an agreement with someone in another company who can take over your obligations if you can't perform them. Include in your emergency plan the name, address, and contact information of that person. Attach a copy of your agreement specifying payment and the other terms you've worked out. Be sure to work out compensation issues carefully. For example, if a colleague handles a matter for your customer, does she keep the entire fee for the work or must she split it with you in a certain manner?

Checklist of Contact Information

To enable your backup to handle the business, provide in your written emergency plan the following key information:

- Names of your business accountant, attorney, bank relationship manager, and insurance agent (including contact information).

- A list of clients or customers and vendors or suppliers.

- Security information (access codes and passwords to computers and security systems, combination to office safe, keys to safe-deposit box).

- Insurance policies (what they cover and where they're kept).

- Signature authorization on company bank accounts. You may wish to require two signatures (other than yours) so that one person can't unilaterally run through the company's money.

Make sure your files are well organized so that those who need access to them can find what they're looking for. Also, make sure your backup knows your current obligations (such as when things must be shipped or services performed). Post this information on a calendar, in a work order, or in another format that can be easily found and followed.

Keep your emergency plan on your computer, but be sure to store a copy at another location away from your business. Make that location known and easily accessible to your family, staff, and other backup personnel.

Security Concerns

Whether your business operates from an office, storefront, factory, or home, think about your security issues. Simple measures can provide great protection for your business in case of disaster.

Computer Systems

Depending on the nature of your business, your computer data may be the heart and soul of your company. At the very least, it contains critical information that you don't want falling into the wrong hands. According to the CERT Coordination Center, a government-funded cybersecurity monitoring agency, Internet attacks increased in 2004 by 40 percent over attacks in 2003. Talk with a computer expert for ways to secure your data. Here are some ideas:

- Use software security packages to block spam, viruses, worms, and other unwanted online intrusions that can adversely affect computer operations.

- Install a firewall to prevent hackers from accessing your system. Cost: about $40.

- Use passwords for computer entry. Change passwords frequently, especially when an employee leaves the company.

Data backup is a key way to protect your information in case of disaster. At least if there is a problem, there is a way to recover your information. There are many ways to handle this important task. If you back up to disk, the simplest method, store backup disks off-site (far from your main location). Other backup methods include tape or backup to alternate systems. Consider using online backup services that automate the process for you (the cost varies with the amount of data you need to back up).

Documents

"Dumpster diving," a practice in which thieves rummage through garbage to find credit card numbers and other vital information that can be used to secure loans or buy goods in other people's names that the thieves never pay for, is a serious problem today. This practice is not limited to consumers; businesses can have their identities compromised as well.

Safeguard your business information. You owe it to your customers to protect their key information that may be included on documents you're disposing of. Put confidential or secret information in files marked clearly as "Confidential" or "Secret." Limit employee access to these files. Keep in mind that 84 percent of lost confidential information is due to employees, and the majority of this is from employees who have left the company, according to International Data Corp.

Properly dispose of unwanted mail such as business credit card offerings, as well as files and other documents you no longer want, including:

- Checks and bank statements.

- Employee information.

- Formulas and trade secret materials.

- Patient information (the Health Insurance Portability and Accessibility Act can expose you to penalties for improperly disposing of patient information).

Buy the right paper shredder for the security level and shredding volume you do. (See Table 12.1.)

If the volume of your paper disposal is substantial, instead of shredding materials yourself, use a company that can do on-site shredding and disposal for you.

Also consider buying a machine that can shred floppy disks, hard CDs, credit cards, and smart cards.

The Premises

Break-ins can be costly—even if you're insured. The insurance may cover the *cost* of goods stolen but can't compensate for the

TABLE 12.1   Paper Shredder Requirements

Security Level	Cut Requirement
Security Level 5 (approved by the U.S. Department of Defense)	Cross-cut $1/32$" × $1/2$"
Security Level 4 (secret documents)	Cross-cut $1/16$" × $5/8$"
Security Level 3 (HIPAA compliance; confidential documents)	Cross-cut $1/8$" × $1 1/8$" or strip-cut $1/16$"
Security Level 2 (sensitive internal documents)	Strip-cut $1/8$" to $1/4$"
Security Level 1 (internal documents)	Cross-cut $3/8$" × $1 1/2$" to $3 1/8$" or strip-cut $3/8$"

time and effort it takes for you to process your claim, replace lost items, and overcome your sense of vulnerability.

Consider installing a burglar alarm system connected to a central monitoring company. Costs start at about $30 per month for monitoring (the initial installation costs vary widely and can be thousands of dollars). Depending on your type of business, surveillance cameras may also be desirable.

Cars, Trucks and Vans

If your business is a to-go operation where you provide services at customer locations, make sure your transportation and what it carries are protected. For example, don't leave tools exposed on truck beds that are unsupervised. Set up procedures for locking up equipment when vehicles are unattended.

Forget about noisy car alarms that provide little protection. When selecting a security system, consider only ones that actually prevent vehicle theft, such as transmission interruption devices.

Business Continuity Plan

You've done what you can to prevent disaster. You've gotten through the disaster itself. Now it's time to recover and get back to business. To make sure that you can do this, it is a good idea to create a business continuity plan (and keep a copy of the written plan off-site so you can access it after the disaster).

Assess Your Options

Don't assume that reopening your business is the only alternative you have. You've survived but your business may not, at least in the same form as before the disaster. As difficult as the decision may be, you may prefer to simply close up shop and start over at another time or at another location, retire, or work for someone else rather than sinking money into an enterprise that may not succeed in the long run. This decision is based on your personal situation (e.g., your age, the predisaster health of your business) as well as what happened to your customers as a result of the disaster. For example, if a disaster has destroyed your customer base, reopening in the same location may not be the wisest course of action.

Recognize that the disaster can be a life-changing event. Take time to make the right decision about your future based on rational information rather than emotion. Consult with your board of advisers or other professionals who can give you an unbiased view on your alternatives.

Reopen Your Doors

If you want to stay in business where you are, then clean up your existing space or, if necessary, find an alternative location at least temporarily. Using professional cleaners may be helpful in this situation.

Recover your computer data from off-site storage facilities. Work with your information technology (IT) professionals to get your systems up and running again.

Contact staff to alert them to time and/or location changes for your business. Work with your staff to make accommodations for their personal issues arising from the disaster. Some employees, for example, may need additional time off to address their issues.

Make Insurance Claims

Contact your insurance company immediately. It will assist you in submitting a claim for damages. Where necessary, submit claims for property damage to pay for repairs as well as claims under a business interruption policy to obtain money to pay expenses such as rent at an alternative site.

Handle Your Stress

Don't underestimate the personal toll that a disaster can have on you and your staff. Recognize the problem and, if necessary, seek professional help.

Recovery without a Plan

If you do not have a business continuity plan and disaster strikes, you can still take immediate action to continue your business activities. Here are some measures to consider:

- *Safety.* Check the conditions of your facilities to make sure they are safe for your staff and customers before recommencing operations. Where necessary, have a building inspector look things over. If there are safety concerns that cannot be remedied immediately, seek an alternative place to operate temporarily.

- *Assess damages.* In order to submit an insurance claim or seek government loans or assistance, you need to document your losses. Create a checklist of the damages you've sustained, including loss of inventory, equipment, and the like. The more detailed your claim, the more likely you can recover for your loss.

- *Clean up.* Damage from storms and fires may be readily cleaned up. Use a professional cleaning service (the cost may be covered by your insurance).

- *Restore services.* In order to operate from your usual location, make sure that power and phone service are restored. Where applicable, also see that sprinkler systems are operational.

- *Make repairs.* Temporary repairs can be sufficient to put you back in operation. For example, if all that is needed is a new window or a roof repair, making these repairs quickly can let you open your doors.

Check Tax Filing Extensions

At a time of disaster the last thing you want to be thinking about is taxes. Fortunately, the IRS may grant additional time to file certain returns if your area is declared a federal disaster area. But no extensions are possible for information returns (e.g., Form 1099s).

The IRS can also waive interest and penalties on income taxes, but it does not have the authority to do so on payroll taxes (although Congress can act, as it did for victims of Hurricane Katrina). So you may have more time to make your estimated tax payments, but you usually must continue to deposit your employment taxes. If you cannot do so, be prepared to pay interest and penalties (another cost of doing business). To learn about federal tax relief, go to www.irs.gov and click on the "Newsroom."

Get Cash from a Tax Loss

If your insurance does not fully cover your property damage incurred in a federal disaster area, you may use your own tax dollars to rebuild. The federal tax law allows you to claim a disaster loss either on the return for the year *before* the year of the disaster or on the return for the year of the disaster. If you opt to claim the loss on the prior year's return, you can apply for a refund by reporting the loss on that return if it has not yet been filed or by filing an amended return.

For more details on tax rules for disaster losses, see IRS Publication 547, *Casualties, Thefts, and Disasters*, Publication 584B, *Business Casualty, Disaster, and Theft Loss Workbook*, and Publication 2194B, *Disaster Losses Kit for Business*, at www.irs.gov. The workbook publication contains a number of schedules (e.g., office furniture and fixtures, information systems, office supplies) that you can use to inventory your property losses.

Long-Term Recovery Actions

Where damage is substantial and insurance does not adequately cover your losses, you may require additional funding to restore your business to its predisaster condition. The American Red Cross and other private organizations usually do not provide assistance to small businesses, but government agencies may help.

Obtain an SBA Loan

After an unprecedented four hurricanes struck Florida and 13 other states in 2004, the Small Business Administration (SBA) approved more than $2.1 billion in disaster loans to about 64,500 residents and business owners in the disaster areas. The SBA response following Hurricane Katrina has not been as dramatic, with approval 67 days after the event of only 593 of the 27,293 loan applications the SBA has received, or less than 2.5 percent.

The SBA provides two types of assistance:

1. *Physical disaster loans* to help restore, repair, or replace damaged property, including inventory, machinery, and equipment. Funds cannot be used to expand or upgrade a business unless state or local authorities require such changes. Keep detailed records of how funds are spent. The maximum loan is $1.5 million, which includes debris removal. Loans of $10,000 do not require collateral; larger loans do. Approval is usually given within one to three weeks from the date of your application.

2. *Economic injury disaster (EID) loans* to provide capital when a disaster renders a business unable to meet its obligations and to pay its ordinary and necessary operating expenses, regardless of any physical damage. The lending limit is $1.5 million. Interest rates are as low as 2.9 percent for businesses and terms are up to 30 years. The amount and term of the loan are set by the SBA, based on your financial condition.

To apply for an SBA disaster loan, go to www.sba.gov and click on "Disaster Recovery."

FEMA Assistance

If your losses occurred in a federally declared disaster area, you may be eligible for help from the Federal Emergency Management Agency (FEMA) (www.fema.gov). The SBA is the main source of disaster recovery funding, but FEMA can direct you to other resources to supplement your insurance recovery and SBA assistance.

Review Insurance Coverage

How well did your existing policies protect you? Where necessary adjust your coverage for greater protection in the event of a future disaster.

Create a New Disaster Recovery Plan

Lightning usually doesn't strike twice, but just in case it does, be prepared. Assess the effectiveness of your disaster planning for the event you've just experienced. With hindsight, what would you have done differently? What would you have done the same? What improvements can you make on your planning and your responses?

LESSONS ABOUT DISASTERS

✔ Recognize that devastating things will happen that can threaten the life of your business.

✔ Create an emergency plan to get you and your staff safely through a disaster.

✔ Create a backup plan in case something happens to you.

✔ Protect your staff, facilities, and computer system from theft and other disasters.

✔ Put your business continuity plan into effect after a disaster.

✔ Review your disaster recovery actions to revise future plans.

INDEX